ENTREPRENEURIAL POWER

ENTREPRENEURIAL POWER

Build Wealth and Live Your Best Life

DARRIN ELFORD

Acknowledgements

Writing this book has been a journey filled with insights, growth, and the support of many incredible people. First and foremost, I want to thank the business leaders who I aspire to emulate and the peers that I have interacted with who have inspired me to write this book. Your challenges, feedback, and wisdom have been invaluable in shaping the ideas I share here.

To my readers: thank you for picking up this book. You're already taking the first step towards becoming a better, more confident business leader and entrepreneur. I hope the tools and insights within these pages empower you to understand yourself and the abilities you have to become a business magnate and build a large business empire.

I also want to express my deepest gratitude to my loved ones who helped turn my ideas into a structured, coherent, and readable book. Your hard work and patience have made this possible, and for that, I am truly grateful.

To my mentors: your guidance, support, and encouragement have shaped my career and helped me refine the concepts I teach. Your influence has been a key part of my growth as both a writer and a teacher.

Finally, to the countless inspirational leaders and executives who have shared their personal experiences with me over the years, thank you. Your stories and struggles have been the fuel for my understanding of this subject, and I am honored to have learned from each of you.

This book wouldn't have been possible without all of you. Thank you for your wisdom, your trust, and your unwavering support.

Table of Contents

Introduction

Becoming a successful entrepreneur is more than just holding a title or managing a company's bottom line. It's about shaping the future, inspiring your team, navigating challenges, and making decisions that will resonate for years to come. In *Entrepreneurial Power: Build Wealth and Live Your Best Life*, I share the principles, insights, and strategies that have helped me—and countless other leaders—thrive in today's fast-paced, ever-changing business world.

In this book, you will find the essential mindset qualities that define great entrepreneurs: resilience, emotional intelligence, strategic vision, and the ability to foster a culture of growth and excellence. You'll learn how to transform your ideas into a real business, the art of scaling up your business for success and discover the tools to create your large business empire. You will learn financial literacy skills, how to streamline systems and processes as well as the importance of building a high-performance team culture.

Each section is filled with practical tips and actions that you can take to build your entrepreneurial skillset and propel you to become a successful entrepreneur. The information is drawn from real-life experiences, case studies, and practical strategies that you can implement immediately to transform both your leadership and your organization. Whether you're at the beginning of your entrepreneurial journey or an experienced entrepreneur seeking to refine your approach, this book offers valuable tools to help you thrive.

As an entrepreneur, your decisions shape not only the future of your company but also the lives of the people who rely on your business success. In the pages that follow, you will be guided through the core competencies that every successful entrepreneur must master.

The journey of entrepreneurship is never easy, but it's one that brings incredible rewards. You are invited to take the lessons in this book, apply them in your own way, and make your mark as a corporate leader who drives lasting success.

Welcome to *Entrepreneurial Power: Build Wealth and Live Your Best Life*—let's get started on your journey to greatness.

1

The Entrepreneurial Mindset

Introduction to the Entrepreneurial Mindset

As you stand at the edge of your entrepreneurial journey, it's important to understand one crucial thing: an idea is not a business. Many aspiring entrepreneurs think that simply having a great idea is enough to launch a successful business. But here's the truth: ideas are a dime a dozen. A business, however, is built from execution, resilience, and mindset.

The Difference Between an Idea and a Business

An idea is a spark of creativity—a concept that excites you and promises potential. But without action, that idea will remain just that: an idea. A business, on the other hand, requires tangible steps, planning, and a relentless drive to bring that idea to life. It's not just about thinking of something clever; it's about turning that thought into something real, something that can serve a purpose, meet a need, and generate value for others.

For instance, you might have an idea for a new app that helps people manage their time better. This is just an idea. To turn it into a business, you need to consider the following:

- Who is your target market?

- What problems does your app solve?

- How will you make money from it?

- What resources will you need to develop it?

An idea alone is not enough to sustain a business. A successful business is the result of thorough research, planning, and hard work.

The Power of Self-Belief and Resilience in Entrepreneurship

Entrepreneurship is not for the faint of heart. You will face challenges, setbacks, and moments where doubt creeps in. But here's where your mindset becomes your biggest asset. The power of self-belief and resilience will be your foundation.

- Self-belief is the inner confidence that you can turn your idea into something real, no matter the obstacles you encounter. Without it, every challenge will feel like a mountain too steep to climb. Belief is the fuel that keeps you going when things seem impossible.

- Resilience is your ability to bounce back from failures, learn from mistakes, and keep moving forward. It's understanding that failure isn't the end—it's part of the process. Every successful entrepreneur has encountered failure, but what separates them from the rest is their ability to get back up and keep going.

In those tough moments, remember: Resilience is not about never falling down—it's about getting up stronger each time you do.

Practical Steps

Self-belief and resilience are the twin engines that will drive you through the highs and lows of your entrepreneurial journey. But just like any skill, they must be developed. The good news is that you don't need to be born with them—they can be nurtured and strengthened through practice. Below are practical steps you can take to build both your self-belief and resilience, so you can thrive as an entrepreneur.

---

1. Start With Small Wins

Building self-belief begins with proving to yourself that you *can* succeed. If you focus on achieving small, manageable goals, you create a pattern of success that boosts your confidence.

- **Set daily goals**: Start by setting small, achievable goals each day. Whether it's completing a task on your to-do list, making one connection with a potential client, or spending an hour learning a new skill, accomplishing these tasks will provide immediate proof of your ability to succeed.

- **Celebrate your wins**: No matter how small the achievement, take time to acknowledge it. Celebrate the fact that you moved one step closer to your goal. This creates a positive feedback loop that reinforces your self-belief.

2. Reframe Negative Thoughts

In the world of entrepreneurship, negative thoughts will inevitably pop up. The key is not to let them take over. Instead, **reframe** these thoughts into something more constructive.

- **Identify negative beliefs**: When you think, "I'm not good enough to run this business" or "I'll fail just like everyone else," pause and acknowledge these as limiting beliefs. Recognize that they are not facts—they are just thoughts.

- **Challenge those beliefs**: Ask yourself: What evidence do I have that I *can* succeed? Focus on your strengths, past successes, and the skills you're building. Replace negative thoughts with more empowering ones like, "I'm learning and growing every day," or "Every failure brings me closer to success."

By challenging your inner critic and replacing self-doubt with positive self-talk, you strengthen your belief in your ability to succeed.

3. Learn From Setbacks

Failure is not the opposite of success—it's a part of it. **Resilience** is the ability to bounce back from setbacks and keep moving forward. When you encounter obstacles, use them as learning opportunities rather than reasons to quit.

- **Analyze what went wrong**: When something doesn't go as planned, take a step back and look at what happened. What can you learn from the experience? Did you miss a crucial step? Was there a flaw in your plan? This reflective process allows you to grow and improve, rather than feeling defeated.

- **Focus on the lessons**: Every setback is a lesson in disguise. Instead of seeing failure as a roadblock, view it as a stepping stone that gets you closer to your goal. This mindset shift builds resilience because you realize that failure is a natural part of the journey and does not define your ability to succeed.

4. Build a Support System

Entrepreneurship can be isolating at times, which is why it's essential to surround yourself with people who uplift and inspire you. A strong support system will help you maintain belief in yourself when things get tough.

- **Find a mentor**: Seek out someone who has walked the path before you. A mentor can offer invaluable advice, guidance, and encouragement. Their belief in your potential can help reinforce your own.

- **Connect with like-minded entrepreneurs**: Whether it's through networking events, online forums, or social media groups, connecting with others who are also pursuing their dreams will help you feel less alone. They can offer advice, share their own stories of resilience, and remind you that you're not the only one facing challenges.

- **Surround yourself with positivity**: People who support you and encourage you to keep going are invaluable. Their positivity will fuel your resilience when the going gets tough.

5. Practice Self-Care

Your mind and body are connected. The stronger and healthier you feel physically, the more resilient you'll be mentally. Self-care is crucial for sustaining long-term motivation and focus.

- **Exercise regularly**: Physical activity is proven to reduce stress, boost mood, and improve overall well-being. Whether it's a quick walk, yoga, or hitting the gym, staying active will help you feel more energized and mentally sharp.

- **Get enough rest**: Entrepreneurship can be demanding, but you must prioritize sleep. A well-rested mind is a productive mind, and it allows you to think clearly and make better decisions.

- **Take breaks**: Don't burn yourself out. Schedule time for relaxation and hobbies that rejuvenate you. A well-balanced life will help you maintain your resilience during stressful times.

6. Visualize Success

Visualization is a powerful tool that successful entrepreneurs use to stay motivated and focused. By imagining yourself achieving your goals, you strengthen your belief that it is possible.

- **Create a vision board**: Gather images, quotes, and reminders of your goals and dreams. Put them on a board that you can see daily. This will keep your dreams alive and serve as a constant reminder of why you're working so hard.

- **Daily visualization practice**: Spend a few minutes each day imagining your success in vivid detail. Picture yourself running a thriving business, interacting with customers, and living the life you want. Feel the emotions associated with this success—pride, joy, and accomplishment. This mental exercise will reinforce your belief in your ability to make it happen.

7. Stay Consistent

Building self-belief and resilience requires consistency. It's not about making huge leaps every day; it's about showing up, even when it feels tough.

- **Create a routine**: Develop daily habits that keep you on track, like setting aside time for planning, networking, learning, or working on your business. Consistency, even in small actions, will gradually build momentum and confidence.

- **Embrace patience**: Building a business is a marathon, not a sprint. Trust that with steady effort, you will see progress. Resilience isn't about pushing through without stopping; it's about staying the course when things get tough and trusting the process.

By practicing these steps, you will gradually cultivate the power of self-belief and resilience that is essential for entrepreneurial success. Remember: success isn't about being fearless—it's about being brave enough to keep going, even when things get tough. The more you believe in yourself and develop resilience, the more unstoppable you will become.

Developing the Confidence to Take the First Step

The first step is always the hardest. The fear of the unknown, the fear of failure, and the fear of making mistakes can hold you back. But here's the secret: no one has it all figured out at the start. Every successful entrepreneur has faced the same fear, and they've all had to start somewhere.

To build the confidence to take the first step, follow these practical strategies:

1. Start Small

   You don't need to launch a massive business right out of the gate. Start with a simple version of your idea, even if it's just a prototype or a small project. Taking small steps will help you gain momentum and build confidence over time. As you see progress, your belief in yourself will grow.

2. Break Down the Big Goal

   Instead of focusing on the daunting task of building an empire, break your vision down into manageable milestones. Ask yourself, "What can I do today to move forward?" These smaller actions will give you a sense of accomplishment and will help you build the confidence to keep going.

3. Surround Yourself with Positivity

   The people you surround yourself with will influence your mindset. Seek out mentors, supportive friends, and like-minded individuals who inspire and encourage you. Avoid negativity or people who doubt your potential. Build a network of individuals who believe in your dream, because their belief will help fuel your own.

4. Learn Continuously

    Knowledge is confidence. The more you learn about your industry, the more capable you'll feel. Read books, take courses, attend seminars, and connect with people who have experience. You'll never know everything, but you can always learn enough to make progress.

5. Celebrate Small Wins

    Acknowledge every step forward, no matter how small it may seem. Whether it's completing a business plan, gaining your first customer, or launching a website, celebrating these wins will help build your confidence and reinforce the fact that you are moving in the right direction.

6. Visualize Your Success

    Take a moment every day to visualize your success. Imagine the life you want to create and feel the emotions associated with that success. Visualization is a powerful tool for boosting confidence because it helps you see the end result, even when you're just starting.

Remember, the first step may feel like a leap into the unknown, but it's the most important one. As you build your belief in yourself and your business, you'll find that the path ahead becomes clearer and the journey more rewarding. Trust in your ability to learn, adapt, and keep going—because that's how empires are built.

Overcoming the Fear of Failure

Fear of failure is one of the most common obstacles standing between aspiring entrepreneurs and success. It's easy to get paralyzed by the "what ifs"—what if my business fails, what if people don't like my product, what if I lose all my money? These fears are natural, but they don't have to control you.

The most successful entrepreneurs in the world didn't get to where they are without facing failure. In fact, **failure** is one of the most important stepping stones to success.

In this section, we'll dive deep into why failure is essential for growth, explore case studies of entrepreneurs who started with little to no knowledge, and provide you with practical steps to overcome the fear of failure and transform it into your greatest strength.

The Importance of Embracing Failure as a Stepping Stone

Failure is often seen as the end of the road, but in reality, it's just part of the process. Every failure you experience is an opportunity to learn and grow. In fact, **failure is not the opposite of success—it's part of it**.

Here's why embracing failure is so important:

- **Failure teaches you valuable lessons**: Every mistake or setback you face is a learning opportunity. It's like taking a test—you don't pass unless you make mistakes and learn from them. Failures reveal what doesn't work, which gives you valuable insight into what will work in the future.

- **Failure builds resilience**: The more you face challenges and keep going, the stronger you become. Overcoming failure builds mental toughness and helps you adapt more quickly to obstacles. Resilience is what keeps you moving forward, even when things get tough.

- **Failure fuels innovation**: Many of the greatest innovations in business came about because someone failed first. Failure forces you to think outside the box, try new things, and innovate in ways that you might not have otherwise. Some of the most successful businesses in history were born out of failure.

Think about it this way: If you never failed, how would you know how to succeed? You wouldn't have the experience or knowledge needed to navigate the challenges of running a business. Failure makes you smarter, more strategic, and better equipped for the next challenge.

Case Studies of Successful Entrepreneurs Who Started with Little to No Knowledge

Let's look at a few examples of successful entrepreneurs who started with little knowledge or experience, faced multiple failures, and eventually built empires.

1. Steve Jobs (Apple)

Steve Jobs is one of the most iconic entrepreneurs of all time. But before he co-founded Apple and revolutionized the tech industry, he was fired from the very company he created. In 1985, after Apple had grown into a multi-million-dollar company, Jobs was ousted in a power struggle. The failure of being fired was devastating, but it didn't stop him.

After leaving Apple, Jobs started **NeXT**, a computer company that failed commercially. He also acquired a little-known animation company called **Pixar**, which eventually became a massive success and was sold to Disney for billions of dollars.

What did Jobs learn from these failures? He learned to innovate, to trust his instincts, and to never give up on his vision. In 1997, Jobs returned to Apple and turned the company into one of the most valuable businesses in the world.

2. Walt Disney

Walt Disney faced many rejections and failures before becoming the household name we know today. Early in his career, Disney was fired from a newspaper job for lacking creativity. His first animation company, **Laugh-O-Gram Studios**, went bankrupt. He was turned down for funding from dozens of investors before finally getting the backing he needed to create **Disneyland**.

Disney's secret to overcoming failure was his belief in the power of his vision and his relentless pursuit of his dreams. He embraced failure, learned from each setback, and kept pushing forward.

3. Richard Branson (Virgin Group)

Richard Branson, the founder of the **Virgin Group**, dropped out of school at 16 and started his first business—a magazine called *Student*. That failed, and he moved on to start a record store, which also faced many challenges. Branson was no stranger to failure, but his passion, persistence, and ability to bounce back made him one of the most successful entrepreneurs in the world.

His philosophy? **"You don't learn to walk by following rules. You learn by doing, and by falling over."** Branson's many failures taught him invaluable lessons about risk, decision-making, and perseverance.

Practical Steps to Overcome the Fear of Failure

Fear of failure is normal, but it shouldn't control you. Here are some practical steps you can take to **overcome the fear of failure** and start using it to fuel your journey toward success:

1. Change Your Mindset About Failure

The first step in overcoming the fear of failure is changing how you view failure. Instead of seeing it as something to avoid, begin to see failure as an opportunity to learn and grow. Every mistake is a lesson that brings you closer to success.

- **Reframe failure**: Rather than thinking "I failed," say to yourself, "I've learned what doesn't work. Now I'm one step closer to figuring it out."

- **Focus on progress, not perfection**: Don't wait for everything to be perfect before taking action. Perfectionism can paralyze you. Instead, focus on progress. Every step forward, no matter how small, is a success.

2. Set Realistic Expectations

Failure often feels like a crushing blow when our expectations are too high or unrealistic. Entrepreneurs can become discouraged when things don't happen quickly, or when their first attempt doesn't succeed. To overcome this, set achievable goals and give yourself permission to fail along the way.

- **Break big goals into smaller, achievable steps**: Instead of aiming for a huge, daunting goal, break it down into manageable tasks. Each small achievement will build your confidence and help you overcome fear.

- **Give yourself room to fail**: Accept that not everything will work perfectly from the start. Failure is part of the process. The important thing is to keep learning and adjusting as you go.

3. Build a Support System

Facing failure can feel isolating, but you don't have to go it alone. Surround yourself with people who support and encourage you. A mentor, a coach, or even a peer group can offer valuable perspective and help you keep going during tough times.

- **Find a mentor**: Seek out someone who has been through the ups and downs of entrepreneurship. A mentor can guide you through the challenges, offer advice, and help you see failure from a healthy perspective.

- **Connect with other entrepreneurs**: Join a network of like-minded individuals who understand the journey. Sharing your struggles and victories with others helps you realize you're not alone, and it keeps you motivated to push through fear.

4. Take Small, Bold Steps

The best way to overcome fear is to take action. The longer you wait, the more the fear grows. Take small, bold steps that move you closer to your goals, even if you're afraid.

- **Start before you're ready**: Don't wait for everything to be perfect before you take action. Start with what you have, and refine things as you go. The sooner you begin, the sooner you can learn and adjust.

- **Embrace calculated risks**: Entrepreneurship requires taking risks, but those risks should be calculated. Weigh the pros and cons, but don't let fear paralyze you from making decisions. The bigger the risk, the bigger the reward.

Conclusion: Failure is Just the Beginning

The most successful entrepreneurs have faced failure, learned from it, and used it to fuel their journey. Embrace failure as part of the process, and let it teach you valuable lessons. With the right mindset, support, and actions, you can overcome your fear of failure and use it as the stepping stone to your success.

Remember, **failure is not the end**—it's simply a pit stop on your way to greatness. So, take that first step, learn from your mistakes, and keep moving forward. You've got this.

Building Mental Toughness and Adaptability

In the world of entrepreneurship, the path is rarely straight. You'll face challenges, setbacks, and moments when everything feels uncertain. The difference between successful entrepreneurs and those who give up is often **mental toughness** and **adaptability**. These traits allow you to navigate obstacles, stay focused on your goals, and keep moving forward, even when things get tough.

In this section, we'll explore how to cultivate a **growth mindset**, the critical role of **adaptability**, and practical steps to develop **mental toughness** so that you can thrive in the face of adversity.

Cultivating a Growth Mindset

One of the key pillars of mental toughness is having a **growth mindset**. This concept, popularized by psychologist Carol Dweck, is the belief that your abilities and intelligence can be developed over time with effort, learning, and persistence. People with a growth mindset embrace challenges, see failures as opportunities to learn, and believe that hard work leads to improvement.

Contrast this with a **fixed mindset**, where individuals believe their abilities are set in stone, and failure is seen as a reflection of their inadequacy. A growth mindset, on the other hand, is empowering because it allows you to see every setback as a stepping stone to success.

How to Cultivate a Growth Mindset:

1. **Embrace Challenges** Instead of avoiding difficult tasks, lean into them. The harder the challenge, the greater the opportunity to learn and grow. Challenge yourself regularly—whether it's by tackling a complicated business problem or stepping outside your comfort zone.

2. **Learn from Criticism** Constructive criticism is a powerful tool for growth. Rather than taking feedback personally, view it as an opportunity to improve. Ask for feedback often and use it to sharpen your skills and enhance your business strategy.

3. **Celebrate Effort, Not Just Results** People with a growth mindset celebrate their efforts, not just their successes. Acknowledge the work you put in, even if the results don't match your expectations. This helps reinforce the idea that progress is more important than perfection.

4. **Persevere Through Setbacks** When things don't go as planned, use the setback as fuel to try again. Remind yourself that failure is not permanent—it's just part of the learning process. The key is to keep going, knowing that each effort brings you closer to your goal.

The Role of Adaptability in Facing Unexpected Obstacles

In entrepreneurship, things rarely go as planned. You might face market shifts, sudden financial challenges, or unexpected competition. The ability to **adapt** is crucial to overcoming these hurdles and thriving despite uncertainty.

Adaptability is your capacity to pivot when necessary, to change strategies in response to new information, and to keep moving forward when things don't go the way you expected. Being adaptable allows you to see problems as opportunities to find creative solutions, rather than roadblocks that will stop you in your tracks.

Why Adaptability is Essential:

- **It helps you embrace change**: The business world is constantly evolving. New technologies, customer preferences, and market conditions can create unexpected challenges. Adaptable entrepreneurs are able to quickly adjust and pivot their strategies to stay competitive.

- **It fosters resilience**: Adaptable entrepreneurs don't waste energy lamenting setbacks. Instead, they focus on finding solutions, adjusting their approach, and staying on course despite obstacles. This resilience is what enables them to weather the storm and continue pushing toward success.

- **It encourages innovation**: When things don't go as planned, adaptability encourages you to think outside the box. This mindset can lead to new ideas, innovative products, or better ways of doing things that you might not have considered if everything went smoothly.

Practical Steps to Develop Mental Toughness

Mental toughness is the ability to stay focused and determined, no matter how tough the circumstances get. It's what keeps you going when things get difficult, and it's what enables you to stay calm under pressure. Building mental toughness doesn't happen overnight, but with consistent effort, you can strengthen your mindset and become more resilient in the face of challenges.

1. Practice Self-Discipline

Mental toughness begins with the ability to control your actions and stay committed to your goals. Self-discipline helps you stay on track even when distractions or temptations arise. Developing this discipline is crucial for entrepreneurship, where staying focused on the bigger picture is essential for long-term success.

- **Create a daily routine**: Establishing a routine helps you stay organized and productive. Set aside time each day to focus on key tasks, whether it's working on your business, networking, or learning new skills.

- **Stay consistent**: It's easy to get sidetracked by new ideas or short-term setbacks. Mental toughness requires consistency—showing up and doing the work, even when motivation is low.

2. Manage Your Stress

Stress is inevitable in entrepreneurship, but it's how you manage it that counts. High levels of stress can lead to burnout, anxiety, and poor decision-making. Learning how to manage stress effectively will keep your mind clear and focused, which is essential for building resilience.

- **Practice mindfulness**: Meditation, deep breathing, and mindfulness exercises can help you stay present and calm under pressure. Even taking a few minutes each day to breathe deeply can help you reset your mind.

- **Take care of your body**: Physical health and mental toughness are closely connected. Regular exercise, a balanced diet, and sufficient sleep help reduce stress and improve your overall resilience.

3. Focus on What You Can Control

When faced with challenges, it's easy to get caught up in things you can't control. However, mental toughness comes from focusing on what you **can** control. This mindset helps you stay positive and proactive, even when things aren't going your way.

- **Identify your circle of control**: Focus your energy on things you have direct influence over—your actions, your attitude, and your work ethic. Let go of the rest.

- **Accept uncertainty**: There will always be unknowns in business. Instead of fearing them, embrace uncertainty as part of the adventure. Cultivate the belief that you can handle whatever comes your way.

4. Set Realistic Expectations and Stay Patient

Mental toughness doesn't mean pushing yourself to the brink of exhaustion. It means knowing when to keep pushing and when to step back. Set realistic expectations for yourself, and understand that success takes time. Be patient with yourself and your business.

- **Set small, achievable goals**: Break down big objectives into smaller, more manageable tasks. Celebrate small wins along the way, and don't rush the process.

- **Practice patience**: Understand that success doesn't happen overnight. Business growth is often slow and steady. Focus on progress rather than instant results.

5. Keep a Positive Inner Dialogue

Your internal dialogue is a reflection of your mindset. The way you talk to yourself can make a huge difference in your ability to persevere through challenges. Replace negative self-talk with encouraging, empowering thoughts that keep you focused on your goals.

- **Affirmations**: Use positive affirmations to remind yourself of your strengths and capabilities. For example, say to yourself, "I am resilient," or "I learn and grow from every challenge."

- **Visualize success**: Spend time each day visualizing yourself overcoming obstacles and achieving your business goals. This mental exercise helps reinforce your belief in yourself and strengthens your mental toughness.

Conclusion

Building mental toughness and adaptability is a continuous process. It requires practice, patience, and a willingness to embrace challenges as opportunities for growth. By cultivating a growth mindset, becoming adaptable to unexpected changes, and following the practical steps outlined here, you can develop the mental resilience needed to thrive as an entrepreneur.

Remember, it's not about avoiding obstacles; it's about how you respond to them. Strengthen your mindset, stay adaptable, and embrace each challenge with confidence. In the end, your mental toughness will be the key to your long-term success.

Developing Vision and Setting Long-Term Goals

One of the most powerful tools in your entrepreneurial toolkit is a strong **vision**. A clear, compelling vision is the North Star that guides you through the highs and lows of building your business empire. However, many entrepreneurs start with only vague dreams or ideas of success—like "I want to be rich" or "I want to change the world." These dreams are important, but they are not enough.

To turn these dreams into reality, you need a **vision** that's specific and actionable. A vision becomes powerful when it is broken down into clear **business objectives**, and when you develop a **roadmap** to achieve those goals over time. In this chapter, we'll walk you through how to transform vague ideas into concrete business goals, and how to build a strategic roadmap that leads you to creating a large business empire.

How to Turn Vague Dreams into Clear Business Objectives

It's easy to dream big when you think about the future, but those dreams need to be turned into clear, actionable **business objectives**. Without specific goals, you may find yourself overwhelmed, lost, or discouraged when things don't go according to plan. That's why it's essential to take your vague dreams and refine them into clear, measurable objectives.

1. Define Your Long-Term Vision

Your vision is the foundation of everything you do in business. It's where you see yourself and your company in the future. To create a compelling vision, you need to ask yourself some key questions:

- **Where do I want my business to be in 10 years?**

- **What kind of impact do I want my company to have?**

- **What values will guide my decisions and actions along the way?**

A large business empire isn't built overnight, so your vision needs to include both short-term and long-term aspirations. A strong vision will not only help you stay motivated, but it will also provide clarity when making business decisions.

For example, let's say your dream is to create a sustainable fashion brand. A specific vision could be: "I want to build a global fashion brand that leads the industry in eco-friendly clothing while making fashion more accessible for everyone." This vision is clear, actionable, and gives you something tangible to work toward.

2. Break Your Vision into Clear, Specific Goals

Once you have a clear vision, the next step is to break it down into specific **business objectives**. These are the steps that will get you closer to turning your vision into reality. To do this, you can use a framework like **SMART goals** (Specific, Measurable, Achievable, Relevant, Time-bound).

Here's how it works:

- **Specific**: Make your goals clear and precise. For example, "I want to generate $1 million in revenue in the first two years."

- **Measurable**: You need a way to track progress. For example, "I will increase my customer base by 20% every year."

- **Achievable**: Your goals should be challenging but possible. Ensure that you have the resources and skills needed to achieve them.

- **Relevant**: Ensure your goals align with your long-term vision and business values.

- **Time-bound**: Set a timeline for achieving each goal. For example, "I will launch my first product within six months."

By breaking down your vague dreams into **SMART goals**, you create clear targets that help guide your decisions and actions along the way.

3. Align Your Daily Actions with Your Business Objectives

With clear business objectives in place, it's time to focus on aligning your daily actions with those objectives. Every day, you should be taking small steps that get you closer to your long-term goals. This could include tasks like:

- Researching your industry

- Developing your product or service

- Building relationships with potential customers

- Marketing your brand

The key is to stay consistent. Success isn't about taking huge leaps every day; it's about making steady, continuous progress.

Creating a Roadmap to Have a Large Business Empire

Now that you've turned your dreams into clear goals, it's time to create a **roadmap** to guide your journey. A roadmap outlines the steps you'll need to take over time to achieve your long-term vision. It serves as your plan of action—an essential tool that keeps you focused and helps you stay on track, even when things get tough.

1. Start with Your End Goal in Mind

Your roadmap begins with your end goal: building a large business empire. However, you can't leap directly to that point—you need to create a series of smaller, strategic goals that build up to your ultimate vision.

Let's break it down:

- **Phase 1: Foundation (Year 1-3)**

  o Focus on building a strong brand and customer base.

  o Develop a minimum viable product (MVP) and gather customer feedback.

  o Set realistic financial goals—what revenue target would represent early success?

  o Create a solid marketing plan to reach your target audience.

- **Phase 2: Growth and Expansion (Year 4-7)**

- Expand your product or service offering to appeal to more customers.

- Focus on scaling operations, such as hiring the right team and improving infrastructure.

- Increase revenue and refine your marketing strategies.

- Start seeking investment or strategic partnerships to fuel growth.

- **Phase 3: Scaling to a Global Empire (Year 8-10)**

  - Scale your business internationally.

  - Look for acquisitions or partnerships that will strengthen your market position.

  - Introduce new products and diversify revenue streams.

  - Ensure your business is well-positioned for a potential IPO (Initial Public Offering) or other major exit strategy.

2. Identify Key Milestones and Metrics for Success

Your roadmap isn't just about the big picture—it's also about tracking progress along the way. To keep your business on track, identify **key milestones** that you want to hit at each stage. These could include:

- Revenue targets (e.g., reaching $1 million in sales by Year 2)

- Customer acquisition goals (e.g., gaining 100,000 users in the first year)

- Product development milestones (e.g., launching your second product by Year 3)

- Market expansion goals (e.g., entering a new country or region by Year 5)

These milestones give you clear targets to aim for, and they help you stay focused and motivated as you move forward. When you hit a milestone, take time to celebrate and adjust your roadmap if necessary.

3. Develop Strategies to Overcome Obstacles

Every journey to building a large business empire will have obstacles. The key is to be prepared for them and adapt along the way. Your roadmap should include strategies for overcoming common challenges, such as:

- **Cash flow issues**: Develop a strategy for managing finances, including fundraising and managing expenses.

- **Competition**: Keep a close eye on competitors and differentiate your brand by emphasizing unique value propositions.

- **Market changes**: Be flexible and ready to pivot if there are shifts in customer preferences or industry trends.

By planning ahead and being ready to adapt, you can navigate unexpected challenges without losing sight of your goals.

4. Continuously Reevaluate and Adjust Your Roadmap

The business world is constantly evolving, and your roadmap needs to evolve with it. As you progress, it's important to continuously evaluate your goals, milestones, and strategies. This allows you to identify what's working, what's not, and where you need to adjust.

- **Track your progress regularly**: Review your goals and milestones every quarter. Are you on track to hit your targets? What needs to be changed?

- **Adapt to new opportunities**: As your business grows, you'll likely encounter new opportunities or challenges. Be open to adjusting your roadmap to take advantage of these changes.

Conclusion

Building a large business empire is not a dream that can be realized without clarity and a strong plan. By turning vague ideas into clear business objectives and creating a detailed roadmap, you'll set yourself on the path to long-term success. Remember, success is a journey, not a destination, and every step you take brings you closer to your vision.

To reach your ultimate goal, stay focused, remain adaptable, and celebrate every small victory along the way. With the right vision, a clear roadmap, and a relentless pursuit of your goals, there's nothing stopping you from building your business empire. Keep going—you're on your way.

2

Turning Your Idea into a Real Business

Identifying Market Gaps and Validating Your Idea

In the world of entrepreneurship, ideas are a dime a dozen. But the real key to success is identifying a gap in the market that needs solving—and validating that your idea has real potential. Let's dive into how you can find that gap and validate your business idea in the most effective way possible.

How to Find the Right Problem to Solve

The first step to building your business empire is identifying the right problem to solve. It's not just about coming up with an idea that excites you, it's about solving a problem that matters to a specific group of people. Here's how you can uncover the right problem:

1. **Observe the World Around You:** Great entrepreneurs are keen observers. Take a step back and look at the world through a critical lens. What problems do people frequently face? Are there inefficiencies or frustrations in daily life, work, or leisure? Sometimes, the best problems to solve are those that you or someone close to you experiences regularly.

2. **Look for Pain Points:** Pain points are the things that cause frustration for people in a given industry or niche. Whether it's too much time spent on a task, unnecessary complexity, or poor customer service, pain points can be your gateway to a great business idea. The key is to identify these pain points and think about how you could simplify or improve them.

3. **Leverage Your Expertise and Passion:** Think about your own expertise, skills, and passions. The problems you are most likely to solve successfully are often tied to your own experiences and knowledge. If you understand a

particular industry deeply or have lived through a specific challenge, you are better positioned to solve those problems with an innovative solution.

4. **Tap into Emerging Trends:** Look for emerging trends in the market—these can be a goldmine for identifying problems that have not yet been addressed. New technologies, societal shifts, or changes in consumer behavior can lead to new problems. By staying ahead of the curve, you can solve problems that others haven't even thought about yet.

5. **Talk to Real People:** The best way to understand what problems people face is to ask them. Talk to friends, family, colleagues, and even strangers. Ask open-ended questions about their struggles, frustrations, and needs. Real-world insights from people who live through the problems you're thinking of solving will provide you with valuable perspectives and ideas.

Conducting Market Research to Validate Your Business Idea

Once you have an idea, the next step is to validate it. Market research is a crucial process that helps you assess whether your idea has legs. You don't want to waste time and resources building something no one wants. So, how do you ensure there's demand for your solution? Let's break it down.

1. **Start with Desk Research:** Begin by researching your industry and competitors. Look for reports, surveys, and studies that provide insights into the market you plan to enter. Use sources like government reports, trade publications, and online resources like Statista or IBISWorld to get an understanding of market size, trends, and growth potential. The more informed you are, the better your decision-making will be.

2. **Analyze Your Competition:** Understand who your competitors are and what they are doing. Study their products, services, pricing strategies, and customer reviews. What are they doing right? Where are they falling short? Identifying gaps in their offerings will give you clues about where you can differentiate and create a better solution.

3. **Survey Your Target Audience:** A direct way to validate your idea is by asking your target audience. Create a survey using tools like Google Forms, SurveyMonkey, or Typeform to gather feedback on your business idea. Ask clear, concise questions such as:

- How much would you pay for this solution?

- What features are most important to you?

- What challenges do you face related to this problem?

The answers will give you direct insights into whether your idea resonates with your target market.

4. **Conduct Interviews:** Surveys can provide useful data, but interviews allow for deeper insights. Speak directly to potential customers in one-on-one conversations. You can ask follow-up questions and get detailed answers. Focus on understanding their needs, challenges, and how they would react to a potential solution.

5. **Prototype and Test Your Idea:** In today's world, you don't have to wait months or years to see if your idea works. Create a simple prototype of your product or service. It doesn't have to be perfect—just enough to give potential customers a sense of what you're offering. Test it with a small group of people and observe their reactions. Their feedback will help you refine your offering.

6. **Use Landing Pages for Early Validation:** A smart, low-cost way to validate an idea is by creating a landing page. This is a simple website that outlines your product or service and includes a call-to-action (CTA), such as asking visitors to sign up for more information or pre-order your product. Tools like Unbounce or Leadpages make it easy to create landing pages. If people are interested enough to sign up or purchase, that's a solid indication that your idea has demand.

7. **Leverage Social Media:** Social media platforms are an excellent tool for testing your business idea. Create posts, run polls, and ask for feedback on platforms like Instagram, Facebook, Twitter, or LinkedIn. Pay attention to the level of engagement and sentiment. Are people excited about your idea? Are they asking for more information or expressing interest in buying it? This feedback will give you a good sense of market interest.

8. **Pilot Programs and Minimum Viable Product (MVP):** Before fully launching your product or service, run a pilot program or release a Minimum Viable Product (MVP). The MVP is the simplest version of your product that solves the core problem. By launching an MVP, you can gather real-

world feedback and make improvements based on actual user experiences before investing heavily in production or marketing.

Conclusion

Finding the right problem to solve and validating your business idea are two of the most important steps you'll take on your entrepreneurial journey. The key to success is not just coming up with a brilliant idea but ensuring that the problem you're solving is real and that your target audience wants a solution. Conducting thorough market research, talking to potential customers, and testing your idea will give you the confidence to move forward with your business. Remember: ideas are important, but validation is everything.

By identifying market gaps and validating your business idea, you're laying the foundation for a strong, successful empire. Now, get out there, do the work, and make sure your idea is built on solid ground!

Creating Your Company Structure

"The structure of your business is the backbone of your empire. Build it right, and everything else will fall into place."

One of the most important decisions you'll make as an entrepreneur is choosing the right business structure. The structure you choose will impact how you operate, how you pay taxes, and how much risk you take on. It can also affect the way you raise money, share ownership, and grow your business. Let's explore the different types of company structures, how to pick the right one, and the pros and cons of each.

Types of Business Structures

There are several types of business structures, each with its own advantages and disadvantages. It is important to remember that each country has its own company structures so you will need to do your research for your chosen country. The main options for the USA are:

1. Sole Proprietorship

- o **What it is:** A sole proprietorship is the simplest and most common type of business structure. It's a one-person business where you, the owner, are in complete control.

- o **Advantages:**
  - Easy and inexpensive to set up.
  - You have full control over decisions.
  - Less paperwork and fewer regulations.
  - All profits go to you.

- o **Disadvantages:**
  - Unlimited personal liability. If your business is sued or takes on debt, you are personally responsible.
  - Harder to raise money or get investment.
  - Limited opportunities for growth.

2. Partnership

- o **What it is:** A partnership is a business owned by two or more people who share responsibilities, profits, and losses. Partnerships can be general or limited.

- o **Advantages:**
  - Easy to set up and more resources than a sole proprietorship.
  - Shared responsibilities and skills, which can improve business operations.
  - More capital available for growth.

- o **Disadvantages:**
  - Partners are personally liable for business debts (in a general partnership).
  - Potential conflicts between partners.
  - Profits must be shared, which could lead to disagreements on how much each person should earn.

3. **Limited Liability Company (LLC)**

   - o **What it is:** An LLC is a hybrid business structure that combines the flexibility of a partnership with the liability protection of a corporation. It's a popular choice for small to medium-sized businesses.

   - o **Advantages:**
     - Limited liability means your personal assets are protected from business debts or lawsuits.
     - Flexibility in management and taxation (you can choose to be taxed as a sole proprietorship, partnership, or corporation).
     - Fewer formalities and paperwork compared to a corporation.

   - o **Disadvantages:**
     - More expensive and complicated to set up than a sole proprietorship or partnership.
     - In some states, there are annual fees or taxes for maintaining an LLC.
     - Limited life span (depending on the state, an LLC may be required to dissolve after a certain period or after a member leaves).

4. Corporation (Inc.)

- o **What it is:** A corporation is a separate legal entity from its owners, offering the most protection in terms of liability. There are two types of corporations: C-corporations (C-corps) and S-corporations (S-corps).

    - **C-Corp:** A traditional corporation that is taxed separately from its owners.

    - **S-Corp:** A corporation that passes income and losses directly to its shareholders, avoiding double taxation.

- o **Advantages:**

    - Limited liability for owners and shareholders.

    - Ability to raise large amounts of capital through the sale of stocks.

    - Perpetual existence—corporations continue to exist even if an owner leaves or passes away.

- o **Disadvantages:**

    - Expensive and time-consuming to set up.

    - Complex regulations and paperwork.

    - Double taxation for C-corporations (the company is taxed on profits, and shareholders are taxed again on dividends).

    - More control by shareholders than by founders.

5. Cooperative (Co-op)

- o **What it is:** A cooperative is a business owned and operated by a group of individuals for their mutual benefit. Profits are typically shared among the members based on their contribution or usage.

- o **Advantages:**
  - Shared decision-making, making it a more democratic structure.
  - Members may receive discounts, services, or dividends based on their participation.
  - Potential for stable, long-term relationships with other members.
- o **Disadvantages:**
  - Less control for individual members.
  - Profits may be shared even if not all members are active contributors.
  - Difficult to attract outside investors.

How to Choose the Right Corporate Structure

Choosing the right structure depends on several factors, including your business goals, the level of liability protection you need, how you plan to raise capital, and how much control you want to have. Here's how to evaluate your options:

1. **Consider Your Liability Risk:** If your business involves high risks (such as operating a restaurant or manufacturing), you may want to choose a structure that protects your personal assets, like an LLC or corporation. A sole proprietorship or partnership doesn't offer this protection.

2. **Evaluate Your Capital Needs:** If you plan to raise a significant amount of capital or offer stock to investors, a corporation is often the best choice. LLCs can also raise money, but corporations have the advantage when it comes to attracting venture capital or investors.

3. **Think About Taxes:** Sole proprietorships and partnerships are taxed once, meaning all income is passed through to the owners and taxed on their personal tax returns. LLCs can choose their tax structure, while corporations may face double taxation unless they are an S-corp.

4. **Level of Control and Flexibility:** If you want complete control over decision-making, a sole proprietorship or a partnership gives you that freedom. Corporations, on the other hand, have shareholders and boards of directors, meaning your control may be diluted.

5. **Growth and Exit Strategy:** If you plan to sell your business in the future or expand it significantly, a corporation might be the right fit because it can easily sell shares and continue to operate even if ownership changes.

Types of Shares and Quantity

When forming a corporation, one important aspect to understand is how shares work. Shares represent ownership in your company, and the number and type of shares you issue can affect how much control you retain and how profits are distributed.

- **Common Shares:** These are the basic shares issued to owners and can be bought or sold. Holders of common shares have voting rights in the company and can receive dividends if the company profits.

- **Preferred Shares:** These shares give holders priority over common shareholders when it comes to receiving dividends and in the event of liquidation. However, preferred shareholders typically do not have voting rights.

- **Authorized Shares vs. Issued Shares:**

  o **Authorized Shares:** The total number of shares a company is legally allowed to issue.

  o **Issued Shares:** The number of shares that have been sold or distributed to shareholders.

The number of shares you choose to issue will depend on how much control you want to retain and how many people you intend to have as investors or owners. Typically, new companies authorize more shares than they issue at first, which gives them flexibility to sell more shares in the future.

Conclusion

Choosing the right company structure is a pivotal decision in your entrepreneurial journey. It affects everything from your day-to-day operations to long-term growth and personal liability. Be sure to weigh the pros and cons of each structure carefully, keeping in mind your business goals, the level of risk you're comfortable with, and your future plans for raising capital and expanding. The right structure will help you build a strong foundation for your business empire, allowing you to focus on what truly matters: growth, innovation, and success.

Creating a Business Plan that Works

"A business plan is your roadmap to success. It's the bridge between your idea and the empire you want to build."

Starting a business without a solid plan is like trying to build a house without blueprints. A business plan is more than just a document you file away. It's a blueprint for your business, outlining your vision, strategy, and how you'll make your dream a reality. A great business plan not only helps you stay focused and organized but also communicates your vision to potential investors, partners, and stakeholders.

In this chapter, we'll walk through the key elements of a winning business plan, dive into financial modeling, and explore practical steps to create a business plan that works.

The Key Elements of a Winning Business Plan

A winning business plan is comprehensive yet clear, providing a detailed outline of your business idea, goals, and strategy. Here are the essential elements every business plan should include:

1. **Executive Summary**

   o **What it is:** The executive summary is a snapshot of your business plan, summarizing the key points. Although it appears at the beginning, it's often written last, after you've figured out all the details.

   o **What to include:**

      ▪ A brief description of your business, its products or services.

      ▪ The problem you're solving and your unique solution.

      ▪ Your target market and why they need your product or service.

      ▪ Your goals and milestones for the next few years.

2. **Company Description**

   o **What it is:** This section provides an overview of your company, including its mission, vision, and structure. It's where you explain who you are and what you stand for.

   o **What to include:**

      ▪ The legal structure of your business (LLC, Corporation, Sole Proprietorship, etc.).

      ▪ Your mission statement—what drives your business and sets you apart.

      ▪ The short- and long-term goals of your company.

3. **Market Research and Analysis**

   o **What it is:** In this section, you demonstrate your understanding of the market you're entering. You outline your target customers, competitors, and industry trends.

- What to include:
  - A description of your target market—who they are, what they need, and where they're located.
  - Analysis of competitors—who they are, what they offer, and how you plan to stand out.
  - Industry trends and potential market opportunities.

4. **Products or Services Offered**
   - **What it is:** Here, you describe the products or services your business will offer and explain how they solve the problems of your target market.
   - **What to include:**
     - Detailed descriptions of each product or service.
     - Unique selling points (USPs) that differentiate your offerings from competitors.
     - Any future plans for product development or expansion.

5. **Marketing and Sales Strategy**
   - **What it is:** This section covers how you plan to attract and retain customers. It outlines your marketing tactics and sales process.
   - **What to include:**
     - Marketing channels you'll use (social media, SEO, paid ads, etc.).
     - Pricing strategy and positioning in the market.
     - Your sales process—how will you convert leads into customers?

6. **Operations and Management**

   o **What it is:** This part describes the day-to-day workings of your business and the team who will run it.

   o **What to include:**

      ▪ The roles and responsibilities of your team members.

      ▪ Organizational structure—who reports to whom and how decisions are made.

      ▪ Operational workflow—how your business will produce and deliver its products or services.

7. **Financial Plan and Projections**

   o **What it is:** This section is crucial to investors and lenders. It lays out your financial strategy, funding needs, and projected revenue and expenses.

   o **What to include:**

      ▪ Financial projections (revenue, expenses, profit margins) for at least the first 3-5 years.

      ▪ A break-even analysis—when will your business start turning a profit?

      ▪ Funding needs—how much money do you need to get started, and where will it come from?

Financial Modelling: Understanding Basic Budgeting, Projections, and Funding Needs

One of the biggest challenges new entrepreneurs face is understanding financial modelling. But don't worry! Financials might seem intimidating at first, but they're essential for guiding your business toward success.

1. **Basic Budgeting**

   o **What it is:** A budget is a plan for how you will allocate your money over time. It helps ensure that you don't overspend and that you're on track to meet your goals.

   o **What to include in your budget:**

     ▪ **Revenue:** How much money do you expect to make from your products or services?

     ▪ **Fixed Costs:** Regular expenses that don't change (rent, utilities, salaries).

     ▪ **Variable Costs:** Costs that change depending on sales volume (raw materials, shipping).

     ▪ **Profit Margins:** The difference between revenue and expenses. It tells you how much money you make after covering costs.

2. **Projections**

   o **What it is:** Financial projections are estimates of your business's future performance. These projections should be based on market research, your budget, and realistic expectations.

   o **What to include in projections:**

     ▪ **Revenue Projections:** Estimate how much revenue you will generate over time. Consider seasonal fluctuations and market trends.

     ▪ **Expense Projections:** Estimate your operating expenses and any other costs (marketing, R&D, etc.).

     ▪ **Cash Flow:** Cash flow shows how money moves in and out of your business. Positive cash flow is essential for staying afloat.

- **Profit and Loss (P&L):** A P&L statement summarizes your revenue and expenses to show whether you're making a profit or a loss.

3. Funding Needs

- o **What it is:** Understanding how much money you need to get your business off the ground and how you'll raise it is crucial for long-term success.

- o **What to include:**

  - How much initial capital do you need to start the business?

  - Will you raise funds from investors, take out loans, or use personal savings?

  - What are your financial goals for the next 3-5 years?

The Lean Canvas Business Plan

Traditional business plans can be long and detailed, but not every entrepreneur needs that level of complexity, especially in the early stages. That's where the **Lean Canvas** comes in—a simplified, one-page business plan that helps you map out the core components of your business in a visual and easy-to-understand format.

The Lean Canvas is made up of 9 key elements:

1. **Problem:** What problem are you solving?

2. **Customer Segments:** Who are your target customers?

3. **Unique Value Proposition (UVP):** What makes your solution unique and valuable?

4. **Solution:** What's your product or service that solves the problem?

5. **Channels:** How will you reach your customers? (Marketing, sales, etc.)

6. **Revenue Streams:** How will you make money?

7. **Cost Structure:** What are the main costs involved in running your business?

8. **Key Metrics:** What metrics will you track to measure success? (Sales, customer growth, etc.)

9. **Unfair Advantage:** What do you have that no one else can replicate? (Patents, exclusive partnerships, unique expertise)

The beauty of the Lean Canvas is that it's quick and flexible. You can constantly update and refine it as your business grows and as you learn more about your customers.

Practical Steps to Writing a Great Business Plan

Writing a business plan doesn't have to be overwhelming. Here's a simple, practical process to get you started:

1. **Start with a Vision:** Think about where you want your business to go in the next 3-5 years. What's your ultimate goal? Write down your vision, then break it down into actionable steps.

2. **Do Your Research:** Understand your market, competitors, and customers. This will provide the foundation for your business plan. Talk to potential customers, read industry reports, and keep up with trends.

3. **Outline the Key Elements:** Using the key elements we discussed (executive summary, company description, market research, etc.), start filling out the sections one by one. Keep it simple, and don't worry about perfection.

4. **Create Financial Projections:** Focus on creating realistic financial projections, budgeting, and funding needs. You don't need to be an expert, but you do need to have a basic understanding of how money flows in and out of your business.

5. **Review and Refine:** Once you've written your plan, review it with trusted mentors, advisors, or potential investors. Get feedback, make improvements, and keep refining it.

Conclusion

A well-crafted business plan is a powerful tool that guides you through your entrepreneurial journey. Whether you opt for a traditional business plan or the leaner Lean Canvas approach, the key is to outline your vision clearly and back it up with solid research and financial projections. With a clear business plan, you'll have a roadmap to follow, attract investors, and set your business up for success.

Now, it's time to take the steps outlined in this chapter and create a business plan that works for you. Build it, refine it, and use it as your guide to turn your business dreams into reality!

Building a Brand Identity

"Your brand is not just your logo or your product—it's the story you tell, the experience you create, and the emotions you evoke. It's how the world sees you and feels about you."

Building a strong brand identity is one of the most powerful ways to ensure long-term success in business. It's more than just colors, fonts, and logos—it's about creating a connection with your customers and standing out in a crowded market. A memorable brand can inspire trust, loyalty, and love from your audience, which in turn drives growth and recognition.

In this section, we'll discuss how to create a memorable brand, craft your brand story, understand the value of customer loyalty, and outline practical steps to help you build a brand identity that lasts.

Creating a Memorable Brand and Developing Your Brand Story

A memorable brand doesn't just sell products or services; it sells an experience and an emotional connection. Think about your favorite brands. What makes them stick in your mind? It's not just the product—they've created an image and a story that resonates with you on a deeper level.

1. Define Your Brand Core

Before you can create a memorable brand, you need to know what your brand stands for. This includes:

- **Your Mission:** Why does your business exist? What's the problem you're solving, and how does your product or service make the world a better place?

- **Your Values:** What principles drive your business? Are you focused on innovation, sustainability, customer service, or community? Your values should align with the audience you're targeting.

- **Your Unique Selling Proposition (USP):** What makes you different from your competitors? Why should customers choose your brand over others?

Having a clear understanding of these elements forms the foundation of your brand identity. Once you know your mission, values, and USP, you can begin to build the story that will connect with your audience.

2. Craft Your Brand Story

Your brand story is the narrative that ties your business's history, mission, values, and purpose together. It's what humanizes your brand and makes it relatable to your customers.

Here's how to create a compelling brand story:

- **Start with Why:** Why did you start your business in the first place? Share the journey—whether it's solving a personal problem, addressing a market gap, or fulfilling a passion.

- **Highlight Challenges and Triumphs:** Every good story has conflict. Talk about the struggles you've faced, how you've overcome them, and how those experiences make your brand stronger.

- **Inspire Your Audience:** A brand story isn't just about you—it's about how your audience relates to what you do. Show how your product or service can help your customers solve their problems and achieve their goals.

Your brand story should be authentic, engaging, and true to your business's core values. A good brand story creates an emotional connection with customers, which leads to brand loyalty.

Understanding the Importance of Brand Value and Customer Loyalty

Your brand isn't just a logo—it's a promise. It's the sum of your reputation, customer experience, and the values you uphold. Understanding your brand's value is essential for building long-term customer loyalty, which is one of the most powerful assets your business can have.

1. The Value of Your Brand

Brand value is the perception customers have of your business, shaped by every interaction they have with your brand. It's not just about quality or price; it's about trust, consistency, and the emotions your brand evokes.

To build brand value:

- **Deliver Consistent Quality:** Your products or services must meet or exceed customer expectations. Quality consistency builds trust and reinforces the positive perception of your brand.

- **Provide Exceptional Customer Service:** Great customer service can be a game-changer. Happy customers are more likely to become repeat buyers and brand advocates.

- **Communicate Your Values:** Let your customers know what you stand for. If your brand values sustainability, social responsibility, or innovation, make it clear. People like to support brands that align with their personal values.

2. Customer Loyalty: The Ultimate Goal

Customer loyalty is when your customers not only keep coming back but also become vocal advocates for your brand. Loyal customers are worth their weight in gold—they're easier to market to, less price-sensitive, and more likely to recommend you to others.

To build customer loyalty:

- **Create a Great Experience:** From the first interaction to the post-purchase experience, ensure your customers feel valued at every touchpoint. A seamless, enjoyable experience keeps customers coming back.

- **Engage and Listen to Your Customers:** Build relationships with your customers by engaging with them on social media, responding to feedback, and showing that you value their input.

- **Offer Loyalty Programs or Rewards:** Loyalty programs that offer discounts, exclusive access, or rewards can incentivize repeat purchases and create long-term relationships.

Loyal customers don't just buy from you—they spread the word, recommend your products, and become your most powerful form of marketing.

Practical Steps to Build a Brand Identity

Now that you understand the theory behind brand building, it's time to take action. Here's a practical guide to help you build your brand identity from scratch:

1. Define Your Brand's Mission, Vision, and Values

Start by defining your brand's purpose. Ask yourself:

- What problem are we solving?

- What makes us different?

- What do we want to stand for?

Your mission and values will serve as the guiding principles for everything you do—from your marketing to your customer interactions.

2. Design Your Visual Identity

Visual identity includes your logo, colors, typography, and design elements. This is what people see first, so it needs to be consistent and aligned with your brand personality.

- **Logo:** Create a logo that's simple, memorable, and reflects your brand's values. Your logo should be versatile enough to work across various platforms.

- **Color Palette:** Choose colors that evoke the right emotions. For example, blue is often associated with trust, while red is seen as energetic and bold.

- **Typography:** Pick fonts that are easy to read and complement your logo and color scheme.

Your visual identity should be used consistently across all marketing materials, website, social media, and packaging.

3. Develop a Consistent Voice and Messaging

Your brand's voice is how you communicate with your audience. It should reflect your personality and values, whether that's professional, friendly, humorous, or inspiring.

- **Tone of Voice:** Decide how you want to speak to your customers. Do you want to be formal and authoritative, or casual and friendly?

- **Messaging:** Make sure your messaging aligns with your brand's mission and values. Whether you're writing blog posts, social media updates, or advertising, keep your messaging consistent across all channels.

4. Build an Engaging Online Presence

In today's digital world, your online presence is vital. Use your website and social media platforms to connect with your audience and build a community around your brand.

- **Website:** Your website should reflect your brand's visual identity, provide useful information, and offer an easy-to-navigate experience. It's often the first impression customers have of your business.

- **Social Media:** Use social media platforms to engage with your audience, share your story, and promote your products or services. Regular posting, interaction, and responding to comments help build a loyal following.

5. Consistently Deliver Value

Building a brand identity isn't a one-time task—it's an ongoing process. You need to continually deliver value to your customers. Whether it's through product innovation, customer service, or community engagement, make sure that every interaction with your brand reinforces the message you want to send.

Conclusion

Building a strong brand identity is one of the most important investments you can make for your business. A memorable brand goes beyond just a logo—it's about creating an emotional connection with your audience, telling a compelling story, and consistently delivering on your promises. By understanding the value of brand loyalty and using practical steps to build your identity, you can create a brand that stands out, earns trust, and drives growth.

Now, it's time to start building your brand identity. Define your mission, craft your story, design your visuals, and deliver an unforgettable customer experience. Your brand is your business's most valuable asset—treat it with the care and attention it deserves.

Securing Initial Funding and Resources

"Every business starts with an idea, but turning that idea into a reality takes resources—money, time, and effort. How you secure that initial funding can be the difference between success and failure."

Starting a business without funding is like trying to drive a car with no fuel—it's simply not going to go anywhere. Whether you're launching a product, building a service, or setting up operations, securing the right funding and resources early on is essential to get your idea off the ground.

In this chapter, we'll dive into the various ways you can secure funding for your business, including bootstrapping, crowdfunding, and venture capital. We'll also discuss the importance of building a **Minimum Viable Product (MVP)** and how to test your idea with real customers to ensure it's worth the investment.

Bootstrapping: Building Your Business with Your Own Money

Bootstrapping means funding your business with your own money or resources. This is often the first option many entrepreneurs consider, especially when they are just starting out and don't have access to outside capital.

Pros of Bootstrapping:

- **Full Control:** You don't have to answer to investors or give away any equity in your business.

- **No Debt:** You avoid the burden of loans or external financial obligations.

- **Flexibility:** You can operate and make decisions without outside influence.

Cons of Bootstrapping:

- **Limited Resources:** You're relying on your own savings, which can restrict how quickly or broadly you can grow.

- **Personal Risk:** If the business doesn't succeed, you risk losing your personal funds.

Bootstrapping is ideal if you have some savings or access to personal loans. It's a good choice for early-stage businesses where you want to test your idea without giving away equity, but it does come with the risk of using your own resources.

Crowdfunding: Turning to the Crowd for Support

Crowdfunding allows you to raise money from a large number of people, typically through online platforms. Websites like **Kickstarter**, **Indiegogo**, and **GoFundMe** make it easier for entrepreneurs to showcase their ideas to potential backers.

Pros of Crowdfunding:

- **Access to Capital:** You can raise funds without giving away equity or taking on debt.

- **Market Validation:** If people are willing to contribute, it's a good sign that there's interest in your product or service.

- **Marketing Power:** A successful crowdfunding campaign can act as an early marketing tool, helping you build a customer base before you even launch.

Cons of Crowdfunding:

- **No Guarantee of Success:** Not every campaign reaches its funding goal, and it can be hard to stand out from the crowd.

- **Time-Consuming:** Running a successful campaign requires time, effort, and effective marketing.

- **Pressure to Deliver:** You must fulfill rewards and promises to backers, which can add pressure on your resources.

Crowdfunding is a great option if you have a compelling product and can effectively promote it to a wide audience. It's a chance to prove there's demand for your idea while raising funds and building a community around your business.

Venture Capital: Attracting Investors for Growth

Venture capital (VC) involves securing funding from investors in exchange for equity or ownership in your business. This option is often sought by startups looking to scale quickly, particularly in tech or high-growth industries.

Pros of Venture Capital:

- **Large Amount of Funding:** VC firms can provide significant financial resources to help your business grow fast.

- **Expertise and Mentorship:** Investors often bring valuable industry knowledge, connections, and business experience.

- **Accelerated Growth:** With access to more funding, you can scale operations quickly and tap into larger markets.

Cons of Venture Capital:

- **Loss of Control:** In exchange for funding, you must give up a portion of ownership in your business. You may have to answer to investors and give up some decision-making power.

- **High Expectations:** VCs often expect rapid growth and may push for aggressive scaling, which can put pressure on your business.

- **Long Timeframe:** The process of raising venture capital can be time-consuming and competitive. It can take months or even years to secure funding.

Venture capital is ideal if you're aiming for significant growth and need substantial financial backing. But be prepared to give up a portion of ownership and control in exchange for that investment.

Building a Minimum Viable Product (MVP) and Testing with Real Customers

No matter how much funding you secure, the key to success lies in having a product that solves a real problem. That's where building a **Minimum Viable Product (MVP)** comes in.

An MVP is a version of your product that has just enough features to be functional and usable by early customers. It's designed to validate your idea and get real-world feedback before you invest in building a full-featured product. The goal is to test your assumptions, learn what works, and iterate quickly.

Why Build an MVP?

- **Save Time and Money:** By starting with a simple version of your product, you avoid spending resources on features customers may not need.

- **Get Feedback Early:** Early users can help you identify bugs, usability issues, and areas for improvement.

- **Prove Market Demand:** An MVP can demonstrate that there is actual demand for your product, which is crucial when attracting investors or securing additional funding.

Practical Steps to Build an MVP:

1. **Define Your Core Idea**

   o What is the main problem your product solves? What's the simplest solution you can provide to address this problem?

   o Focus on the core features that make your product unique and valuable.

2. **Map Out the User Journey**

   o Understand how your customers will interact with your product. What steps will they take to use it? How can you make that process as simple and intuitive as possible?

3. Build a Prototype or Simple Version

- o Start by creating a simple prototype or a basic version of your product. If you're building an app, you might begin with just one key feature. If it's a physical product, focus on getting the essential functionality right.

4. Test with Real Customers

- o Launch your MVP to a small group of customers or early adopters. This could be friends, family, or individuals who fit your target market.

- o Gather feedback—what do they like, what don't they like, and what features do they think are missing?

5. Iterate and Improve

- o Use the feedback to make improvements. Maybe customers need more clarity on how to use your product or have suggestions for new features. Keep improving your product based on real-world input.

6. Measure Success and Learn

- o Track key metrics like user engagement, customer retention, and any other data that will show how your MVP is performing.

- o Use this information to make informed decisions about how to proceed with the next version of your product.

Conclusion

Securing initial funding and resources is an essential step in turning your business idea into reality. Whether you bootstrap, crowdfund, or seek venture capital, there are multiple ways to fund your startup based on your goals and the stage of your business.

At the same time, building a Minimum Viable Product (MVP) and testing it with real customers ensures that you're not just building a product in a vacuum, but rather something that people actually want and need. By focusing on core features, gathering feedback, and improving iteratively, you can ensure your business is set up for success from the start.

Remember, securing funding is just the beginning. The real work lies in proving your product's value, building a loyal customer base, and scaling your business sustainably. Stay focused, keep testing and learning, and your business will be on the path to success.

3

Scaling Up – A High Growth Company

Building the Right Team

"A great team is the backbone of every successful business. It's not just about skills; it's about shared vision, collaboration, and trust."

As an entrepreneur, your business will never be able to grow or succeed without the right team. A strong, motivated team will bring your vision to life, tackle challenges head-on, and push your business forward. But how do you build that team? How do you find the right people and foster an environment where they thrive?

In this section, we'll discuss how to identify key roles, hire talent that aligns with your vision, and create a company culture that fosters innovation, collaboration, and success. We'll also cover practical steps to ensure your team is set up for long-term success.

Identifying Key Roles and Hiring Talent That Shares Your Vision

The first step in building the right team is identifying the key roles that are essential for your business. As a founder, it's important to recognize that you can't do everything alone, and it's likely you won't have the expertise in every area of your business. This is where building a strong team becomes crucial.

1. Defining Key Roles in Your Business

Every business has its unique needs, but there are some common roles that most businesses require:

- **Operations:** Someone to handle day-to-day operations, logistics, and ensure that everything runs smoothly.

- **Marketing and Sales:** You need people who can get the word out about your business, create compelling marketing campaigns, and convert prospects into customers.

- **Finance:** You'll need someone to keep track of your cash flow, manage your budget, and handle any financial planning and reporting.

- **Product Development/Service Delivery:** If you're offering a product or service, this role involves developing and refining your offerings to ensure quality and customer satisfaction.

- **Customer Support:** A team dedicated to answering questions, solving problems, and ensuring your customers have a positive experience.

Once you've identified the core roles needed to run your business, the next step is to hire people who align with your vision and values.

2. Hiring Talent that Shares Your Vision

When you hire for your business, it's easy to focus just on technical skills. Of course, you need people who are good at what they do, but it's equally important to hire people who share your vision for the business. When your team is aligned with your mission, they'll be more passionate, motivated, and invested in your company's success.

Here are some steps to ensure you're hiring talent that fits your culture:

- **Look Beyond the Resume:** Technical skills are important, but cultural fit is just as crucial. During interviews, ask questions that reveal a candidate's values, work ethic, and alignment with your company's mission. For example, ask, "What excites you about our company?" or "How do you approach problem-solving in a team setting?"

- **Hire for Passion:** Passion can often outweigh experience. Look for individuals who are genuinely excited about your business and are eager to contribute to your success. A passionate team member will put in the extra effort and drive your business forward.

- **Prioritize Team Players:** Collaboration is key in a small, growing business. Look for candidates who work well in teams, communicate effectively, and are willing to support each other. A team that works together will be much more productive than a group of individuals who don't get along.

- **Be Transparent About Expectations:** Make sure that you clearly communicate the role's responsibilities, the company's goals, and what you expect from each team member. Transparency helps avoid misunderstandings and ensures everyone is on the same page.

Creating a Company Culture That Drives Innovation and Success

Once you have the right people on board, the next step is to create a company culture that encourages innovation, collaboration, and long-term success. Your culture shapes how your team operates, interacts, and contributes to the business.

1. Foster a Collaborative Environment

A collaborative work culture encourages teamwork, idea-sharing, and mutual support. This is essential for a growing business, where everyone needs to pitch in and contribute to different aspects of the operation.

To build a collaborative environment:

- **Encourage Open Communication:** Make sure everyone feels comfortable sharing ideas and feedback. Open communication helps catch problems early, brainstorm solutions, and keep everyone on the same page.

- **Promote Cross-Department Collaboration:** Foster relationships between different teams so that they work together and share insights. For example, marketing and sales teams can collaborate on lead generation strategies, while customer service can share valuable feedback to help improve the product.

- **Host Regular Meetings:** Regular team meetings, one-on-ones, and brainstorming sessions create a space for collaboration. These meetings can be used to align on goals, discuss challenges, and celebrate successes.

2. Create a Culture of Innovation

For your business to thrive, it needs to be adaptable and forward-thinking. Fostering a culture of innovation encourages employees to think creatively, try new ideas, and solve problems in fresh ways.

- **Encourage Experimentation:** Let your team know that it's okay to take risks and experiment with new ideas. Failure can be a valuable learning experience, and you want to create a safe environment for people to try new things.

- **Reward Creativity:** Recognize and reward employees who come up with innovative solutions or ideas that push the company forward. This encourages a mindset of continuous improvement.

- **Provide Learning Opportunities:** Invest in your team's growth by providing opportunities for skill development, training, or attending conferences. When employees feel supported in their growth, they'll be more motivated to contribute new ideas to the company.

3. Establish Core Values and Lead by Example

Your company's values set the tone for the entire organization. These values should reflect your business's core beliefs, how you want to treat your employees, customers, and the world. When everyone knows and lives by the same set of values, it creates a strong sense of unity and purpose.

As the leader, it's important that you embody these values. If you expect your team to be transparent, collaborative, and innovative, you must demonstrate those behaviors yourself. Your actions as a leader will set the standard for your employees to follow.

Practical Tips for Building the Right Team

Now that you understand the theory behind team building and culture, let's get practical. Here are some actionable tips to help you build the right team for your business:

1. Start Small, Scale Smartly

In the early stages, you don't need to hire a huge team. Focus on hiring key individuals who will wear multiple hats. As your business grows, you can start to add specialists to cover specific roles.

2. Be Strategic in Your Hiring

Instead of filling positions quickly, take your time to hire the right people. Consider their long-term potential, and make sure they're excited about your business vision. Conduct thorough interviews and check references to ensure they're a good fit.

3. Create a Positive Work Environment

People perform best when they feel respected and valued. Create a positive work environment where employees feel supported, challenged, and appreciated. Small gestures, like recognizing hard work or celebrating milestones, can go a long way.

4. Encourage Feedback and Adaptability

A business is constantly evolving, so your team needs to be flexible and open to change. Encourage feedback from your employees on how things are going and what can be improved. This makes them feel heard and involved in the company's growth.

5. Lead with Empathy

Empathy is a key leadership trait. When your team feels understood and valued, they're more likely to be loyal, motivated, and productive. Listen to your employees, understand their challenges, and offer support when needed.

Conclusion

Building the right team is one of the most important steps in your entrepreneurial journey. A great team doesn't just work for you; they work alongside you to bring your vision to life. By identifying key roles, hiring talent that shares your values, and creating a company culture that encourages collaboration and innovation, you'll be setting your business up for long-term success.

Remember, a strong team is a reflection of strong leadership. Be intentional with your hires, invest in your people, and lead by example. Your team is your greatest asset—treat them as such, and they will help you build the business empire of your dreams.

Marketing and Sales Strategies for Rapid Growth

"Marketing and sales are the engines that drive your business forward. If you want rapid growth, you need the right strategies in place to reach your customers, build relationships, and convert leads into loyal fans."

No matter how great your product or service is, your business won't grow unless people know about it. This is where marketing and sales come in. These two pillars work together to spread awareness, attract customers, and generate revenue. But how do you scale your efforts effectively? How do you establish a strategy that brings in customers and turns them into repeat buyers?

In this chapter, we'll discuss how to develop effective marketing tactics that will fuel rapid growth, from digital marketing to PR. We'll also look at how to scale your sales operations and establish strategic partnerships that help you expand your reach. And most importantly, we'll dive into practical marketing and sales strategies you can implement right away.

Effective Marketing Tactics for Growth

Effective marketing helps your business stand out from the competition, attract potential customers, and build lasting relationships. Let's take a closer look at the top strategies you can use to achieve this:

1. Digital Marketing: Reaching Your Audience Where They Are

Digital marketing encompasses all the ways you can promote your business online. The beauty of digital marketing is that it's cost-effective and measurable, which means you can track the return on investment (ROI) of each effort.

Some key digital marketing tactics include:

- **Social Media Marketing:** Platforms like Facebook, Instagram, LinkedIn, Twitter, and TikTok offer businesses the ability to engage with their audience directly. Use these platforms to post regular content, run ads, and interact with customers. It's a great way to build awareness and create a community around your brand.

- **Search Engine Optimization (SEO):** SEO helps your website appear in search engine results when people search for keywords related to your business. Focus on optimizing your website's content, including blog posts, product descriptions, and landing pages, to rank for terms your customers are likely to search for.

- **Paid Ads (PPC):** Pay-per-click (PPC) ads on platforms like Google, Facebook, and Instagram allow you to target your ideal customer based on specific criteria, like age, location, or interests. These ads help you drive traffic to your website and generate leads.

- **Email Marketing:** Email campaigns are a great way to nurture relationships with existing customers and convert leads into paying customers. Build a subscriber list and send out newsletters, product updates, special offers, and more to keep your audience engaged.

2. Content Strategy: Tell Your Brand's Story

Content marketing is all about creating valuable, informative, and engaging content that attracts and educates your audience. Content can take many forms, such as blog posts, videos, infographics, podcasts, and eBooks. It's essential to build a content strategy that aligns with your business goals.

Here's how you can leverage content:

- **Blogging:** Create blog posts that address common problems or questions your target audience has. Not only does this position you as an expert, but it also improves your SEO and drives organic traffic to your site.

- **Videos:** Videos are highly engaging and can increase conversion rates. You can create explainer videos, product demos, or even behind-the-scenes content to humanize your brand.

- **Lead Magnets:** Offer free resources like eBooks, whitepapers, or checklists in exchange for your visitors' email addresses. This helps you build your email list and generate leads.

- **User-Generated Content:** Encourage your customers to share their experiences with your brand through reviews, social media posts, and testimonials. This builds trust and acts as social proof for potential customers.

3. Public Relations (PR): Building Credibility and Trust

Public relations (PR) is a strategy for managing how your business is perceived by the public. It's an important way to build credibility, trust, and recognition for your brand. Here are some PR strategies you can implement:

- **Media Outreach:** Reach out to journalists, bloggers, and media outlets to get featured in news articles or interviews. This helps increase your visibility and position your business as an industry leader.

- **Press Releases:** Whenever your business achieves a significant milestone—whether it's launching a new product, raising funds, or winning an award—issue a press release. This helps generate buzz and informs your audience of important developments.

- **Influencer Marketing:** Partnering with influencers who have a following in your niche can increase brand awareness and trust. Influencers can share your product with their audience, and their endorsement can lend credibility to your brand.

Scaling Your Sales Operations

Once your marketing is attracting customers, it's time to focus on scaling your sales operations. You need to set up processes and systems to handle the increased volume of leads and transactions.

1. Build a Sales Funnel That Converts

A sales funnel is the journey your customers take from awareness to purchase. To scale your sales, it's essential to have a structured funnel in place. Here's how you can do that:

- **Top of Funnel (TOFU):** This is where potential customers first discover your brand. Use content marketing, SEO, and digital advertising to capture their attention.

- **Middle of Funnel (MOFU):** Once leads have shown interest, it's time to nurture them. Offer value through educational content, free trials, or discounts. Your goal is to build trust and guide them closer to making a purchase.

- **Bottom of Funnel (BOFU):** This is where customers are ready to make a decision. Provide testimonials, case studies, or time-limited offers to help them commit to purchasing your product or service.

2. Automate Your Sales Processes

As your business grows, you won't have time to manually handle every sale. Sales automation tools can help you streamline and optimize the sales process.

- **CRM (Customer Relationship Management) Software:** Use tools like Salesforce or HubSpot to manage leads, track customer interactions, and automate follow-up emails.

- **Automated Email Campaigns:** Set up email sequences that send timely, targeted messages to your leads based on their actions. For example, after someone downloads an eBook, send them a follow-up email offering a free consultation or product demo.

- **Lead Scoring:** Implement a lead scoring system to prioritize your sales efforts. This system can rank leads based on their level of engagement or likelihood to convert, helping your sales team focus on high-value opportunities.

3. Expand Your Reach with Strategic Partnerships

Strategic partnerships are one of the fastest ways to scale your business. By collaborating with other businesses, you can access new customer bases, share resources, and create win-win scenarios for both parties.

- **Affiliate Marketing:** Set up an affiliate program where partners promote your product or service in exchange for a commission on sales. This allows you to tap into their audience and grow your customer base.

- **Co-Branding Opportunities:** Partner with complementary businesses to create joint marketing campaigns or co-branded products. This helps you expand your reach while offering value to both audiences.

- **Distribution Partnerships:** Work with established distributors to get your product into retail stores, online platforms, or international markets. This can help you rapidly expand your reach without the overhead of setting up your own distribution channels.

Practical Marketing and Sales Strategies You Can Adopt

Here are some actionable marketing and sales strategies you can adopt right now to start driving growth:

1. **Create a Content Calendar:** Plan out your content ahead of time. Create a monthly calendar for blog posts, social media updates, and email campaigns. Consistency is key to keeping your audience engaged.

2. **Leverage Paid Ads:** Run small-scale paid ad campaigns on platforms like Google or Facebook. Focus on a specific demographic to get the best return on investment (ROI). Start with a small budget and test what works.

3. **Optimize Your Website:** Make sure your website is user-friendly, mobile-optimized, and has clear calls to action (CTAs) to drive conversions. A fast, responsive site will improve user experience and boost your SEO.

4. **Use Social Proof:** Showcase testimonials, customer reviews, and case studies on your website and in your marketing materials. Social proof builds trust and helps potential customers feel confident in their decision to buy.

5. **Ask for Referrals:** Don't be afraid to ask satisfied customers for referrals. Offer incentives, such as discounts or free products, to encourage them to spread the word about your business.

6. **Monitor Analytics:** Use tools like Google Analytics, social media insights, and email campaign reports to track your marketing performance. Use this data to make informed decisions about where to focus your efforts.

Conclusion

Marketing and sales are the lifeblood of your business, and to achieve rapid growth, you need to implement strategies that attract, convert, and retain customers. By leveraging digital marketing, content strategies, PR, and scaling your sales operations, you can create a sustainable growth engine for your business.

Don't forget the importance of strategic partnerships, automation, and constant learning as you scale. The right strategies, combined with a proactive mindset, will help you accelerate your growth and build the business empire you've always dreamed of.

Mastering Operations and Streamlining Systems

"The key to scaling your business is building efficient operations. When your systems work smoothly, you free up time to focus on growth and innovation."

As your business grows, it becomes increasingly important to master your operations and streamline your systems. The more efficient your operations, the easier it will be to scale. This doesn't just mean reducing costs—it also means creating a system that allows your business to grow without running into major roadblocks.

We'll dive into how you can improve operational efficiency through automation, outsourcing, and scaling logistics. We'll also explore how to build an infrastructure that will grow with your business. Plus, we'll provide practical steps you can take to streamline your systems and operations so you can focus on what matters most: growing your business.

Operational Efficiency: Automation, Outsourcing, and Scaling Logistics

Efficiency is about doing more with less—whether it's time, money, or resources. When you can streamline your operations, you free up valuable resources to put toward growing your business. Let's look at three key areas to focus on when aiming for operational efficiency: automation, outsourcing, and scaling logistics.

1. Automation: Making Your Business Run on Autopilot

Automation can save you hours of time, reduce human error, and help you scale faster without the added complexity of hiring additional employees. There are countless tasks within your business that can be automated, allowing you to focus on higher-level decisions and strategy.

- **Marketing Automation:** Tools like Mailchimp, HubSpot, or ConvertKit allow you to automatically send emails based on customer actions (like signing up for your newsletter, downloading a guide, or making a purchase). This can nurture leads and keep customers engaged without requiring manual intervention.

- **Sales Automation:** CRM (Customer Relationship Management) systems like Salesforce or Pipedrive can automate parts of your sales process, such as sending follow-up emails, scheduling meetings, or tracking sales activities.

Automating your sales pipeline will help you close more deals with less effort.

- **Accounting and Finance Automation:** Tools like QuickBooks or Xero can help automate your invoicing, expense tracking, and financial reporting. By setting up recurring invoices and automatic payments, you can ensure your finances run smoothly without manual input.

- **Customer Support Automation:** Chatbots or helpdesk software like Zendesk can handle common customer queries 24/7, allowing your team to focus on more complex issues. You can also create automated responses for frequently asked questions on your website.

2. Outsourcing: Leveraging External Expertise

While it's tempting to do everything yourself, it's important to know when to bring in outside help. Outsourcing allows you to focus on growing your business while experts handle specialized tasks. Outsourcing is a great option for functions that are outside your core expertise, or tasks that aren't essential to your day-to-day business operations but still need attention.

- **Administrative Tasks:** Virtual assistants can handle scheduling, emails, data entry, customer service, and other time-consuming administrative duties. This allows you to free up your time to focus on more important matters.

- **Marketing and Content Creation:** If you don't have the skills or time to create content, consider outsourcing blog writing, social media management, or even graphic design. Hiring experts in these areas can improve the quality of your content and allow you to focus on strategy.

- **IT Support:** As your business grows, you may need specialized help with your website, software, or IT systems. Outsourcing IT support to experts can prevent costly mistakes and ensure that your systems remain secure and functional.

- **Manufacturing and Fulfilment:** If you're selling physical products, you can outsource manufacturing and fulfilment to third-party companies (such as a fulfilment center or manufacturer) to handle production and shipping.

This will help scale your business without needing to invest in your own warehouse or equipment.

3. Scaling Logistics: Building Efficient Supply Chains

As your business grows, you'll need to scale your logistics to keep up with demand. Logistics includes everything from inventory management to shipping and delivery. Here are some ways to streamline your logistics:

- **Inventory Management Software:** Tools like TradeGecko or ShipBob can help you track your inventory in real-time. With automated stock level alerts and order tracking, you can reduce the risk of running out of stock or overstocking, helping you make smarter purchasing decisions.

- **Streamline Your Shipping Process:** Work with reliable shipping partners like UPS, FedEx, or DHL, and set up partnerships that provide discounts as your shipping volume increases. You can also integrate your e-commerce platform with your shipping provider to automatically generate shipping labels and track orders.

- **Warehouse Solutions:** If your business requires physical inventory storage, consider outsourcing your warehousing needs to a third-party logistics (3PL) provider. This allows you to avoid the overhead of managing your own warehouse and enables you to scale your inventory as demand increases.

Building Infrastructure That Can Grow with Your Business

To handle growth, you need to build an infrastructure that can scale alongside your business. Infrastructure refers to the systems, tools, and processes that support the day-to-day functions of your business. It includes everything from software tools to communication channels to physical spaces. Building the right infrastructure ensures that your business can handle increased demand and complexity without breaking down.

1. Invest in Scalable Technology

As your business grows, your technology needs will grow with it. Start with tools that are easy to use and can scale as your operations expand. Choose software that can handle larger volumes, more users, and additional features as needed.

- **Cloud-Based Software:** Cloud platforms like Google Drive, Dropbox, and Microsoft 365 allow your team to access files and collaborate from anywhere. This is crucial if you plan to have remote employees or expand globally.

- **Project Management Tools:** As you scale, it becomes essential to keep track of tasks and projects across different teams. Tools like Asana, Trello, or Monday.com help you manage workflows, assign tasks, and stay on top of deadlines.

- **Accounting Systems:** Choose an accounting platform that can grow with your business. QuickBooks, Xero, and FreshBooks allow you to add more features as your needs change, such as payroll, invoicing, and tax reporting.

2. Standardize Your Processes

One of the best ways to streamline your operations is by standardizing your processes. When you have a consistent way of doing things, it reduces errors, improves efficiency, and makes it easier to train new team members.

- **Create Standard Operating Procedures (SOPs):** Write down step-by-step instructions for how common tasks are completed in your business. Whether it's handling customer service requests, processing orders, or running marketing campaigns, SOPs provide clarity and consistency.

- **Automate Routine Tasks:** Look for tasks that can be automated to save time and reduce human error. Automating things like appointment scheduling, invoicing, and reporting will allow your team to focus on more impactful activities.

3. Plan for Future Growth

Don't just think about where your business is today—plan for where it's going. Whether you plan to expand your product offerings, enter new markets, or increase your staff, your infrastructure needs to be able to support that growth.

- **Scalable Systems:** Choose systems that allow for easy integration and expansion. For example, your CRM system should be able to handle a growing customer base, and your accounting software should be able to manage larger volumes of transactions as your revenue increases.

- **Flexible Staffing:** As your business grows, so will your team. Consider using temporary or part-time staff during busy periods to reduce overhead. As you scale, you may want to invest in more permanent hires to support long-term growth.

Practical Steps to Streamline Systems and Operations

Now that we've covered key concepts, let's discuss some practical steps to streamline your systems and operations:

1. **Audit Your Current Operations:** Start by analyzing your current workflows and identifying inefficiencies. Look for tasks that take up too much time or resources, and consider how you can streamline or automate them.

2. **Start Small with Automation:** Begin automating simple tasks first, such as email marketing or social media posting. Once you see the benefits, you can move on to automating more complex processes.

3. **Outsource Non-Core Tasks:** Look at what tasks are essential to your business growth and which ones can be handled by external experts. Outsourcing allows you to focus on scaling your core business.

4. **Invest in Scalable Tools:** Choose technology that can grow with your business. Cloud-based software, CRM systems, and project management tools can be easily scaled as your team and operations expand.

5. **Document Your Processes:** Create clear, written procedures for your team to follow. This helps maintain consistency as your business grows and ensures that every team member is aligned on best practices.

6. **Track Performance:** Regularly monitor your systems and processes to see if they're meeting your efficiency goals. Use data and feedback to continuously improve your operations.

Conclusion

Mastering operations and streamlining systems is essential for any entrepreneur looking to scale their business. By embracing automation, outsourcing, and building scalable infrastructure, you can create a foundation that allows your business to grow smoothly.

The key is to continually improve, adapt, and optimize your operations so that you're always one step ahead. With efficient systems in place, you'll be able to focus on growing your business and achieving your long-term goals.

Funding and Managing Cash Flow During Growth

"Growth is exciting, but without solid financial management, it can quickly become a challenge. To sustain and scale your business, managing cash flow and securing the right funding are essential."

As your business grows, the need for cash becomes even more pressing. Whether you're expanding your team, increasing inventory, or investing in new technologies, the funds required to fuel this growth can quickly outpace your available cash flow. Yet, without a steady stream of money coming in, even the most successful ventures can struggle.

In this section, we'll explore how to navigate the challenges of funding during periods of rapid growth, and how to manage and optimize cash flow to ensure your business can thrive. We'll also dive into practical steps you can take to manage cash flow effectively as an entrepreneur.

Navigating the Challenges of Funding During Rapid Growth

As your business accelerates, the funding needs will grow too. During periods of rapid expansion, the cash requirements for inventory, hiring, marketing, and operations can spike. At the same time, if your revenue isn't growing fast enough, you could face a funding gap. Here's how to navigate these challenges.

1. Understand the Different Types of Funding Options

When funding needs arise, there are several options available, but each comes with its own set of considerations.

- **Bootstrapping:** Many entrepreneurs begin by funding their businesses with personal savings or by reinvesting profits. While this gives you full control over your business, it limits the amount of capital you can access and can put your personal finances at risk.

- **Bank Loans and Credit Lines:** Traditional bank loans or lines of credit are common funding sources, but they require strong credit histories and come with strict repayment schedules. These can be a good option if you need a lump sum of capital for expansion.

- **Venture Capital (VC) and Angel Investors:** For businesses with high growth potential, venture capitalists or angel investors can provide significant funding. In exchange, you give up equity in your business. This is ideal if you need substantial funding and are willing to share control of your company.

- **Crowdfunding:** Platforms like Kickstarter or GoFundMe allow you to raise money directly from your customers. This not only provides funding but also serves as a way to test the market and validate demand for your product or service.

Understanding which type of funding suits your needs and growth stage is crucial. But no matter how you fund your business, remember that managing cash flow is equally important once you've secured that money.

Managing and Optimizing Cash Flow to Fuel Expansion

Cash flow is the movement of money into and out of your business. Positive cash flow allows you to pay your bills, invest in growth, and keep the business running smoothly. Negative cash flow means your expenses exceed your revenue, putting your business at risk.

During periods of rapid growth, managing cash flow can be tricky. Increased sales can be great, but they often come with increased costs. You may need to invest heavily in inventory, new hires, or marketing campaigns—all while waiting for customers to pay their bills. The key to ensuring continued growth is to manage cash flow proactively.

1. Track Your Cash Flow Closely

It's vital to keep a close eye on your cash flow at all times. This means monitoring both your cash inflows (money coming in) and outflows (money going out).

- **Set Up Cash Flow Forecasts:** Create a simple cash flow projection for the next 3-6 months. Include anticipated revenue, expenses, and any potential gaps where cash might be tight. This will help you anticipate problems before they occur and take action early.

- **Use Accounting Software:** Tools like QuickBooks, FreshBooks, or Xero can automate cash flow tracking, making it easier to stay on top of payments, invoices, and financial reports. This gives you a real-time picture of your cash position.

2. Speed Up Payments and Reduce Collection Times

The longer customers take to pay their invoices, the more pressure it puts on your cash flow. Delays in payment can lead to cash flow gaps that slow down your growth. Here's how you can speed up payments:

- **Send Invoices Promptly:** The faster you invoice, the faster you get paid. Send invoices immediately after you deliver a product or service to avoid unnecessary delays.

- **Offer Early Payment Discounts:** Encourage clients to pay sooner by offering a small discount (e.g., 2% off) for early payments. This incentivizes timely payments and can improve your cash flow significantly.

- **Set Clear Payment Terms:** Make sure your payment terms are clear from the start. Specify the payment deadline (e.g., "Net 30," meaning the payment is due 30 days after the invoice date), and enforce them. If clients are consistently late, consider adjusting your terms or requiring upfront deposits.

- **Follow Up on Overdue Payments:** Don't wait until a payment is seriously overdue to remind customers. Send gentle reminders, and if needed, set up automated reminders through your accounting software.

3. Reduce and Control Expenses

As your business grows, it's easy to let expenses spiral out of control. Managing your costs is crucial to keeping cash flow steady. Here are some ways to keep expenses in check:

- **Negotiate Better Terms with Suppliers:** If your business relies on suppliers for inventory or raw materials, negotiate better payment terms or discounts. For example, ask for longer payment terms (e.g., 60 days instead of 30 days) or bulk pricing discounts.

- **Outsource When Possible:** Outsourcing tasks such as customer service, content creation, or IT management can save you money on hiring full-time staff and allow you to focus on core business functions.

- **Reduce Operational Waste:** Look for inefficiencies in your operations, whether it's energy usage, excess inventory, or underutilized staff. Small improvements in efficiency can add up to big savings.

4. Build a Cash Flow Cushion

Building up a cash reserve for your business is one of the best ways to ensure smooth cash flow during growth. A buffer of cash can help you handle unexpected expenses or slow-paying customers without disrupting your operations.

- **Save for a Rainy Day:** Aim to save enough to cover at least 3-6 months of operating expenses. This will give you the confidence to make decisions without constantly worrying about short-term cash flow problems.

- **Set Aside Profits for Growth:** As your business becomes more profitable, consider setting aside a portion of profits for reinvestment into the business or building your cash cushion. This ensures that you always have capital available to take advantage of growth opportunities.

5. Consider Financing When Necessary

Sometimes, rapid growth demands more cash than your business can handle. If you're facing a cash shortfall, consider financing options that don't burden your business with too much debt.

- **Short-Term Loans or Lines of Credit:** A line of credit or short-term loan can help you cover expenses during slower months or while waiting for customer payments to come in. Just be careful to use this option strategically, as borrowing too much can create debt problems.

- **Invoice Financing:** If you have outstanding invoices, invoice financing can help you unlock cash by selling those invoices to a lender. This allows you to get immediate cash flow without waiting for customers to pay.

- **Equity Financing:** If you need a larger amount of funding, consider offering equity in your business to investors. While this means giving up some ownership, it can provide the capital you need to fuel expansion without taking on debt.

6. Monitor Your Key Financial Metrics

Tracking important financial metrics can help you make informed decisions about your business's cash flow. Some key metrics to keep an eye on include:

- **Days Sales Outstanding (DSO):** This measures how long it takes for your customers to pay their invoices. A higher DSO can indicate that customers are slow to pay, which can impact your cash flow.

- **Current Ratio:** This is a measure of your business's ability to cover short-term liabilities with short-term assets. A ratio above 1 means you have enough assets to cover your liabilities, while a ratio below 1 may signal cash flow issues.

- **Cash Conversion Cycle:** This measures how long it takes your business to convert its investments in inventory and other resources into cash from sales. The shorter the cycle, the quicker you can turn sales into cash flow.

Conclusion

Funding and managing cash flow during periods of rapid growth is one of the biggest challenges for entrepreneurs. As your business expands, maintaining a steady cash flow is crucial to ensuring you can continue to grow without hitting financial roadblocks.

By closely tracking your cash flow, speeding up payments, controlling costs, building a financial cushion, and leveraging financing options strategically, you can navigate the growing pains of expansion with confidence. Keep your cash flow in check, and you'll set yourself up for long-term growth and success.

Remember, growing a business is a marathon, not a sprint. Managing cash flow effectively will give you the breathing room you need to fuel your expansion and achieve your vision.

4

Your New Business Empire

Diversification and Legacy Building

"Your business is just the beginning of your empire. Thinking beyond your current success can lead to long-term growth and a legacy that lasts for generations."

As an entrepreneur, you've already proven that you can build and grow a business from the ground up. But the real power lies in thinking beyond the business. This chapter is about expanding your empire and building a legacy—ensuring that your business not only thrives today but also remains strong in the future. We'll explore how to diversify your business, expand internationally, and how to lay the groundwork for a lasting legacy.

Expanding Your Empire: Acquisitions, New Product Lines, and International Growth

Growth doesn't have to stop at your current business model. In fact, the most successful entrepreneurs look beyond their core business to find new ways to scale and add value. There are many strategies for expanding your empire, but they all require a mindset shift—from running a single business to managing multiple revenue streams. Here's how you can expand your empire:

1. Acquisitions: Expanding Through Buying Other Businesses

One of the most effective ways to rapidly scale your empire is through acquisitions. This involves purchasing other businesses that complement or align with your current operations. Here's how you can start:

- **Identify Complementary Businesses:** Look for businesses that can add value to your current operations. For example, if you own a tech company, you could acquire a software development firm to broaden your product offerings. Think about how an acquisition can help you fill a gap or reach a new market segment.

- **Due Diligence:** Before acquiring a business, conduct thorough due diligence. This means reviewing financial records, understanding the business's customer base, and evaluating the company's assets and liabilities. Acquiring a business is a significant investment, so it's crucial to assess the risks and rewards.

- **Integrate the Acquisition Smoothly:** After the acquisition, focus on integrating the new business into your operations. This might involve merging teams, streamlining processes, or aligning the company's brand with your own. Successful integration is key to realizing the full value of the acquisition.

2. New Product Lines: Expanding What You Already Offer

Another powerful way to grow your business is by introducing new products or services to your existing customer base. Expanding your product lines allows you to leverage your current brand loyalty and reach new markets. Here's how you can diversify your product offerings:

- **Understand Customer Needs:** Listen to your customers and identify gaps in your current product offerings. This could be as simple as introducing complementary products that customers are already asking for. For example, a clothing retailer could add accessories or footwear to their collection.

- **Test New Ideas:** Before launching a full-scale product line, test new ideas with a small group of customers. Use focus groups, surveys, or pre-launch campaigns to gauge interest and get feedback.

- **Leverage Existing Channels:** Use your established sales channels, such as your website, social media platforms, and distribution networks, to promote your new products. This will save you marketing costs and make the introduction of your new products more seamless.

3. International Growth: Going Global

Taking your business to international markets is one of the most exciting ways to expand your empire. Global growth allows you to tap into new customer bases and diversify your revenue streams, but it also comes with challenges. Here's how to approach international expansion:

- **Research Foreign Markets:** Identify countries where there's a demand for your product or service. Research the cultural, legal, and economic environment to ensure your product is well-suited for the market. You may need to adapt your product, marketing, or even packaging to cater to local tastes.

- **Partner with Local Experts:** Entering a new international market can be tricky without local knowledge. Partnering with local distributors, agents, or businesses can help you navigate the regulatory environment and expand your brand's presence.

- **Start Small and Scale:** Don't jump into too many international markets at once. Start by focusing on one or two countries, and as you grow, expand into other regions. By scaling gradually, you can better manage your resources and minimize risks.

The Importance of Building a Legacy and Thinking Generationally

Building an empire is not just about making money. It's about creating something that lasts—something that can be passed on to future generations. The true power of entrepreneurship lies in its ability to create lasting value, not just for yourself, but for your family, community, and society as a whole.

1. Defining Your Legacy

A legacy is more than just financial success. It's about the impact you leave on the world, your industry, and the people around you. When you think generationally, you begin to ask yourself:

- **What values do I want my business to represent?**

- **How can I create a positive impact on society?**

- **How can my business continue to thrive after I'm no longer involved?**

Building a legacy is about setting your business up in a way that will continue to prosper, even after your active role has diminished. Here's how to start thinking about your legacy:

- **Establish Strong Values:** Create a company culture and values that align with your vision. A business built on strong ethical values is more likely to endure in the long term, even if leadership changes.

- **Focus on Long-Term Sustainability:** Make decisions today that will benefit the business long into the future. Whether that's investing in innovation, focusing on sustainability, or improving customer loyalty, the key is to ensure your business remains relevant and resilient over time.

- **Mentorship and Education:** Help others learn from your journey. By mentoring future leaders in your business or industry, you can ensure that your knowledge, values, and vision live on.

2. Transitioning Your Business to the Next Generation

If you're thinking about passing your business on to the next generation, it's essential to have a clear plan in place. Here's how to ensure a smooth transition:

- **Prepare Your Successor:** If you intend to pass your business on to your children or another family member, begin grooming them for leadership from an early stage. Allow them to take on more responsibility as they grow into the role.

- **Create a Succession Plan:** A clear succession plan outlines how leadership will transition, who will take over key roles, and how decisions will be made during the handover. This helps avoid confusion and conflict when the time comes.

- **Diversify Ownership:** Consider diversifying ownership by involving other family members, business partners, or even employees. This can help maintain a balance of power and ensure that the business doesn't rely on one individual for its survival.

Practical Actions to Diversify Your Business

Diversifying your business can seem daunting, but it's a crucial step in ensuring long-term growth and stability. Here are some practical steps you can take to start diversifying your business:

1. Identify New Revenue Streams

Look for ways to add new revenue streams to your business. This could include:

- **Subscription models**: Offering products or services on a recurring basis.

- **Licensing**: Licensing your brand or intellectual property to other businesses.

- **Consulting or Services**: Expanding into services related to your product or expertise.

2. Start Small and Test

Diversification doesn't mean jumping into everything at once. Start small by testing new products, services, or markets with minimal investment. Use customer feedback and data to adjust before making larger commitments.

3. Partner with Other Brands

Strategic partnerships allow you to tap into other businesses' customer bases and strengths. Look for companies with complementary offerings and explore joint ventures, co-branding opportunities, or affiliate programs.

4. Leverage Technology and Innovation

Technology can play a huge role in diversifying your business. Invest in new tools or software that can help you reach new customers or automate parts of your business to increase efficiency and reduce costs.

5. Invest in Research and Development (R&D)

Innovation is key to staying competitive and diversifying your offerings. Set aside resources for R&D to develop new products, improve existing ones, or explore new business models. Keeping your business ahead of the curve ensures long-term growth.

Conclusion

Thinking beyond the business is essential for creating a lasting empire. By diversifying your revenue streams, expanding your business through acquisitions or new product lines, and thinking globally, you can fuel your growth and expand your reach. At the same time, focusing on building a legacy and thinking generationally ensures that your success lasts for years to come.

Remember, your business is more than just a company; it's a platform for creating lasting change and wealth for the future. Build wisely, diversify strategically, and always keep an eye on the long-term vision of your empire. Your legacy is waiting to be built—take the steps today to make it happen!

Becoming a Visionary Leader

"As an entrepreneur, you've learned to hustle, build, and grow. But to truly scale your business and create something monumental, you need to shift your mindset from entrepreneur to visionary leader."

Building a successful business is only the beginning. As your company grows, your role as the leader must evolve. Moving from a hands-on entrepreneur to a visionary leader is a critical shift, one that allows you to lead your company with foresight and long-term strategy. You'll need to think not just about the next step, but about where you want your business to go years into the future.

This section will guide you through the transition to becoming a visionary leader. We'll explore how to maintain innovation, sustain your company's competitive edge, and inspire your team to follow your vision.

Shifting from Entrepreneur to Visionary Leader

When you first start your business, you're doing everything—building the product, serving customers, managing operations. This is the entrepreneurial grind. But as your business grows, the day-to-day responsibilities start to shift. You can't be everywhere at once. To succeed in the long term, you need to transition from being just an entrepreneur to a visionary leader who sets the course and guides the company forward.

1. Expand Your Thinking Beyond the Immediate

As an entrepreneur, your focus is on survival—getting through the day, closing sales, and managing immediate challenges. But as a visionary leader, your thinking must broaden. You must focus on long-term goals, setting your company on a course that aligns with your ultimate mission.

- **Develop a long-term vision:** Look at where you want your company to be in 5, 10, or 20 years. What are the values, goals, and milestones that define your success? Your vision should be bold but realistic, providing direction while allowing flexibility for growth.

- **Make strategic decisions:** Every decision you make as a leader should align with this long-term vision. Whether it's expanding into new markets, investing in technology, or recruiting talent, always ask, "How does this fit into the bigger picture?"

- **Delegate operational tasks:** As your role shifts, it's critical to delegate day-to-day responsibilities. Hire strong managers who can handle the operational side of the business while you focus on the big picture.

2. Cultivate a Strong Leadership Team

A visionary leader knows that they can't accomplish their goals alone. Building a strong leadership team is crucial for executing your vision and carrying the company forward. Your team must be empowered to make decisions and execute strategies with your long-term goals in mind.

- **Hire the right people:** Surround yourself with leaders who share your vision and have complementary skills. Look for individuals who bring diverse perspectives, experience, and talents to the table.

- **Trust and empower your team:** As a visionary leader, you must trust your team to execute your vision. Provide them with the resources, guidance, and autonomy they need to succeed, and then step back to allow them to lead their areas.

- **Foster collaboration and communication:** Build a culture of open communication where your leadership team shares ideas and insights freely. A collaborative team can tackle challenges more effectively and contribute to innovation.

How to Maintain Your Company's Innovation and Competitive Edge

A great vision is only as good as its execution. To maintain your company's innovation and competitive edge, you must create an environment where creativity thrives and your business is constantly adapting. As a visionary leader, it's your job to ensure that your company stays ahead of the curve and continues to innovate.

1. Lead by Example: Embrace Innovation

Innovation starts at the top. If you're not open to new ideas and constantly seeking ways to improve, your company will stagnate. Here's how to lead by example:

- **Stay curious:** Be passionate about learning. Read books, attend industry events, and network with other leaders to stay on top of trends and best practices. Encourage your team to do the same and create a culture of continuous learning.

- **Challenge the status quo:** Always ask, "Is there a better way?" Encourage experimentation and push boundaries. By challenging the norms, you inspire your team to think outside the box and create breakthrough ideas.

- **Foster a growth mindset:** Encourage your team to view failures as opportunities for growth, not setbacks. When mistakes happen, lead with understanding and look for lessons learned rather than assigning blame.

2. Create an Innovation-Friendly Culture

The best companies are built on a foundation of creativity and innovation. As a visionary leader, it's your job to cultivate this environment. You want to create a culture where employees feel inspired to think big, challenge themselves, and contribute new ideas.

- **Encourage open dialogue:** Create platforms for team members to share ideas and feedback, whether it's through brainstorming sessions, team meetings, or even informal chats. Make sure everyone feels heard.

- **Reward creativity and risk-taking:** Celebrate employees who come up with innovative solutions or take calculated risks to move the company forward. This reinforces the behavior you want to see across the organization.

- **Allocate time and resources for innovation:** Set aside dedicated time for teams to focus on new ideas, products, or services. Encourage them to explore possibilities without the pressure of immediate deadlines.

3. Stay Adaptable to Market Changes

The business world is always evolving, and what worked yesterday may not work today. As a visionary leader, you need to be flexible enough to pivot when necessary and position your company for future success.

- **Monitor industry trends:** Stay informed about what's happening in your industry and the broader economy. Use this information to make informed decisions and adjust your strategy when needed.

- **Invest in technology and automation:** Technology is key to staying competitive. Invest in tools and systems that streamline your operations, improve customer experiences, and increase productivity.

- **Embrace change:** Don't fear change—embrace it. Whether it's adjusting your product offerings, entering a new market, or restructuring your team, adaptability is a sign of strong leadership.

Practical Actions to Become a Visionary Leader

Now that we've discussed the broader concepts of visionary leadership, let's look at some practical steps you can take to become the visionary leader your company needs:

1. Create a Clear, Inspiring Vision

clear vision is the cornerstone of visionary leadership. Take the time to write down your long-term goals, what your company stands for, and where you want to take it. Then, communicate that vision consistently to your team so everyone is aligned and motivated.

2. Invest in Personal Development

Visionary leaders are lifelong learners. Invest in yourself by attending leadership courses, reading books on strategy and innovation, and seeking mentorship. Your growth as a leader directly impacts the growth of your business.

3. Set Big, Bold Goals

Visionary leaders aren't afraid to set audacious goals. These stretch your limits and inspire your team to think bigger. Break down these big goals into smaller, achievable milestones to track progress and maintain momentum.

4. Foster a Culture of Innovation

Encourage your team to think creatively and reward innovative thinking. Provide them with the freedom and resources they need to experiment and develop new ideas.

5. Focus on Long-Term Sustainability

Don't get distracted by short-term wins. Always ask yourself, "How does this decision fit into our long-term vision?" Keep sustainability in mind, whether it's financial stability, employee well-being, or environmental impact.

6. Lead with Empathy and Purpose

Finally, visionary leaders are empathetic and lead with purpose. Understand your team's needs, care about their well-being, and ensure they see the bigger picture of what you're building together. When your team feels supported and inspired, they'll be more motivated to follow your vision.

Conclusion

Becoming a visionary leader requires a shift in mindset—from focusing on daily tasks to focusing on long-term strategy, from working in the business to leading the business. The most successful entrepreneurs evolve into visionary leaders who inspire their teams, foster innovation, and build companies that stand the test of time.

By embracing your role as a visionary leader, you can ensure that your company not only survives but thrives in a constantly changing world. Remember, leadership is about guiding your team toward a shared future, and your vision will be the compass that leads them there.

Exit Planning and Preparing for IPO or Sale

"As an entrepreneur, building a successful business is a remarkable achievement. But an equally important aspect of entrepreneurship is knowing when and how to exit. A strategic exit can secure your financial future, allow you to move on to new opportunities, and ensure your business continues to thrive."

Many entrepreneurs focus on growing their business but don't give enough attention to the endgame—the moment when they decide to exit the business. Whether you're looking at an Initial Public Offering (IPO), an acquisition, or simply transitioning out of your day-to-day role, strategic exit planning is essential. A successful exit plan can help you maximize the value of your business, protect its long-term stability, and ensure it operates smoothly without your involvement in every detail.

This section will discuss how to prepare your business for an IPO or sale, the key steps in strategic exit planning, and practical actions you can take to ensure a seamless transition.

Preparing Your Business for an IPO or Acquisition

When you've built a strong business, the possibility of an IPO or acquisition becomes a natural next step. However, transitioning from being a private company to a public one (through an IPO) or selling your business to another company (acquisition) is a significant process. Here's how to prepare for each:

1. Preparing for an IPO

An IPO is when a private company offers shares to the public for the first time. It's a complex, multi-step process that requires financial transparency, regulatory compliance, and investor confidence. Here's how you can start preparing:

- **Get Your Financial House in Order:** Public companies are required to disclose their financial performance, so having accurate and up-to-date financial statements is critical. You need strong accounting practices and audits that meet regulatory standards. If your accounting systems are not already compliant with public company standards, it's time to make that change.

- **Develop a Strong Leadership Team:** Investors want to see that a company is managed by capable, experienced leaders. Make sure your management team is solid, with a clear organizational structure and a track record of success. Your leadership team will be scrutinized by investors, so ensure you have the right people in place to manage the business after the IPO.

- **Ensure Legal and Regulatory Compliance:** Going public means your business will be under greater regulatory scrutiny. Prepare by reviewing all your contracts, intellectual property, and corporate governance practices. You'll need a legal team to ensure compliance with securities regulations and the listing requirements of your exchange.

- **Create a Compelling Investor Narrative:** You must craft a compelling story to attract investors. This includes highlighting your company's growth potential, market positioning, and competitive advantages. The better you can communicate why your company will succeed in the long term, the more attractive your IPO will be.

2. Preparing for Acquisition

In an acquisition, your company is bought by another business. This could be a strategic acquisition (where the buyer wants to add your products, services, or market share) or a financial acquisition (where the buyer sees your company as a profitable investment). Here's how you can prepare for a sale:

- **Maximize Business Value:** Before selling, you need to maximize the value of your business. Look for ways to streamline operations, reduce costs, and improve profitability. Buyers will look closely at financial performance, so ensure you're showing your business at its best. This might involve trimming unnecessary expenses, improving margins, or optimizing operational efficiency.

- **Prepare a Comprehensive Data Room:** A data room is a secure online space where all the important documents about your company are stored. It includes financial statements, contracts, intellectual property, employee agreements, and other important legal documents. A well-organized data room helps a potential buyer quickly assess the value and health of your business.

- **Find the Right Buyer:** Not all buyers are created equal. Whether you're looking for a strategic buyer (who wants to integrate your business into their own) or a financial buyer (who is looking for a profitable asset), you need to identify potential buyers who align with your company's values and vision.

- **Negotiate a Fair Price:** It's essential to understand the value of your business before entering negotiations. Work with advisors, such as investment bankers or M&A consultants, to help you get the best price and terms for your sale. You need to know what your company is worth and be prepared to negotiate the terms of the deal.

The Steps to Ensure Your Business Operates Effectively Without You

One of the biggest challenges of preparing for an exit—whether it's an IPO or acquisition—is ensuring that your business can operate smoothly without your constant involvement. Buyers and investors are looking for businesses that can run effectively without the founder having to micromanage every detail. Here are some key steps to ensure your business runs like a well-oiled machine:

1. Develop Strong Systems and Processes

The more automated and efficient your business operations are, the more attractive it will be to potential buyers or investors. To reduce reliance on your direct involvement, create systems and processes that ensure the business runs smoothly on its own.

- **Document Your Operations:** Create standard operating procedures (SOPs) for key functions like customer service, product development, marketing, and sales. These documents should provide clear instructions on how to perform tasks consistently and effectively.

- **Automate Where Possible:** Use technology to automate repetitive tasks. This could include customer relationship management (CRM) systems, email marketing automation, inventory management, or financial reporting. Automation reduces the chances of human error and ensures consistency.

- **Create Clear Job Roles:** Ensure every team member has a clearly defined role and knows their responsibilities. This reduces confusion and keeps things running without constant oversight. When your staff knows what's expected of them, they can operate with greater independence.

2. Build a Strong Management Team

One of the best ways to ensure your business operates without you is by building a reliable and capable management team. This team should be made up of experienced leaders who can make decisions and run the day-to-day operations of the business.

- **Hire Leaders, Not Just Managers:** Make sure your key employees have leadership qualities and are capable of thinking strategically. Managers may handle day-to-day tasks, but leaders are essential for driving the business forward.

- **Empower Your Team:** Provide your team with the authority to make decisions within their areas. Trust them to execute your vision while allowing them to be autonomous. Empowering your leaders builds a stronger, more independent organization.

- **Set Clear Goals and Metrics:** Ensure that your team understands the company's goals and what success looks like. Use key performance indicators (KPIs) to track progress and hold people accountable. By setting clear expectations, you reduce the need for constant oversight.

3. Build a Succession Plan

In preparation for your exit, create a succession plan that outlines how leadership will transition when you step away. A solid succession plan reassures potential buyers and investors that the company can thrive after you're no longer involved.

- **Identify Future Leaders:** Look within your company for individuals who have the potential to take on larger roles. Start grooming them for leadership by providing mentorship, training, and additional responsibilities.

- **Cross-train Employees:** Cross-training employees ensures that key roles can be filled if someone leaves or takes on a new responsibility. Having multiple people who understand each function will keep the business running without disruptions.

- **Prepare for Change:** Transitioning out of a business you built can be emotionally challenging. Start preparing yourself and your team for the changes ahead. Having a well-thought-out plan will help everyone adjust more smoothly.

Practical Actions for Strategic Exit Planning

To ensure that your exit strategy is successful, take these practical steps in your planning process:

1. Start Early

Exit planning is not something you can do overnight. Begin your exit strategy planning early—ideally, years before you intend to sell or go public. This gives you time to increase the value of your business, streamline operations, and find the right buyer or investor.

2. Hire Advisors and Experts

Consult with financial advisors, legal professionals, and M&A experts who can guide you through the complex process of an IPO or acquisition. Their expertise will help you navigate the challenges and maximize the value of your business.

3. Focus on Maximizing Value

Before you exit, focus on maximizing the value of your business. This could mean improving profitability, increasing market share, or building a strong brand presence. Buyers and investors are looking for companies that are positioned for long-term success.

4. Plan for the Future Beyond the Exit

Exit planning isn't just about selling your business. Think about what you want to do after the sale or IPO. Whether you plan to start a new business, invest in other ventures, or retire, having a clear plan for the future will help you transition smoothly.

Conclusion

Strategic exit planning is a critical step in the life cycle of any successful business. By preparing your business for an IPO or acquisition, creating strong systems, and developing a management team that can operate independently, you ensure that your business will thrive even after you step away.

Remember, the exit strategy you choose can have a major impact on your financial future, so plan wisely, take the necessary actions, and ensure a smooth transition that secures both your legacy and your financial success. Your exit is not the end—it's the beginning of new opportunities and chapters in your entrepreneurial journey.

Sustaining Long-Term Success

"Reaching the top is just the beginning. True success is about maintaining momentum, innovating continually, and making a positive impact for the long haul."

As an entrepreneur, you've worked hard to build your business. You've faced challenges, overcome obstacles, and achieved the success you've always dreamed of. But here's the truth: reaching the top is not the end—it's just the beginning of a new journey. The real challenge is sustaining long-term success and continuing to grow, evolve, and make an impact over time.

We will guide you through strategies to sustain your business for the long run. We'll explore how to keep innovating, growing, and reinvesting to secure your place in the market. Plus, we'll talk about the importance of giving back to your community as part of your journey to lasting success.

How to Keep Innovating and Growing Even After Reaching the Top

Many entrepreneurs think that once they've reached a level of success, their business will run itself. But the most successful entrepreneurs know that growth and innovation are ongoing processes. The world is always changing, and so must your business. Here's how you can keep innovating and growing, even after you've reached the top:

1. Keep a Growth Mindset

Success can sometimes lead to complacency, but maintaining a growth mindset is crucial. Instead of seeing your achievements as the final destination, view them as milestones on a continuous journey.

- **Learn from your failures:** Failure is often the best teacher. When something doesn't go as planned, take time to learn from it. Analyzing setbacks and mistakes allows you to grow and adapt quickly.

- **Stay curious:** Always ask questions and look for ways to improve. Stay curious about trends in your industry, new technologies, and evolving customer preferences. Curiosity fuels innovation.

- **Keep challenging yourself:** Even when you've reached a comfortable position, continue setting new and bigger goals. Stretch yourself beyond what seems achievable. This keeps the entrepreneurial fire alive and ensures continued growth.

2. Foster a Culture of Innovation Within Your Team

Innovation isn't just about what you do as the leader—it's also about creating an environment where your team feels empowered to innovate. A team that is encouraged to think outside the box and take risks will help drive growth and maintain your competitive edge.

- **Encourage creativity:** Give your team the freedom to experiment with new ideas, products, or services. Create opportunities for brainstorming sessions, and reward creative thinking. Allow them to explore new concepts without fear of failure.

- **Invest in research and development:** Whether it's through creating new products, improving existing ones, or researching market trends, allocate resources toward R&D. Innovation often comes from exploring areas you haven't tapped yet.

- **Embrace collaboration:** Foster a culture where departments work together. When sales, marketing, product development, and customer service collaborate, they bring diverse perspectives that can lead to innovative solutions.

3. Diversify and Expand

To sustain long-term success, don't put all your eggs in one basket. Diversifying your offerings or expanding into new markets can provide additional revenue streams and help weather any changes in the industry.

- **Introduce new products or services:** Look for gaps in the market that align with your brand. Expanding your product line or service offerings keeps your customers engaged and opens doors to new opportunities.

- **Explore new markets:** Consider geographic expansion, entering international markets, or targeting a new customer demographic. Expanding your reach allows your brand to tap into fresh opportunities and increases your chances of long-term success.

- **Acquisitions and partnerships:** Strategic acquisitions or partnerships with other businesses can help you diversify and increase your influence. Look for businesses that complement your existing offerings or have access to new audiences.

The Importance of Reinvesting and Giving Back to Your Community

Sustaining long-term success goes beyond just profits—it's also about making a positive impact on the world around you. As your business grows, so should your responsibility to reinvest in the community that helped you get to where you are. Giving back is a powerful way to build a legacy, gain goodwill, and maintain a purpose-driven business.

1. Reinvest in Your Business

One of the most powerful ways to sustain success is by reinvesting back into your business. Instead of simply taking profits out of the company, use some of that capital to fuel the next stage of growth.

- **Invest in technology and infrastructure:** As your business grows, your systems and processes need to scale with it. Invest in technology, automation, and infrastructure to streamline operations and improve efficiency.

- **Develop your team:** Your people are your greatest asset. Invest in employee development through training programs, leadership courses, or mentorship opportunities. A skilled, motivated team will drive continued success.

- **Enhance customer experience:** Continuously invest in improving the customer experience. Use feedback from customers to upgrade products, optimize services, and make your brand more appealing to your target market.

2. Give Back to the Community

Sustaining long-term success isn't just about your business; it's also about creating a positive impact in the world. Giving back to the community not only helps others but also strengthens your brand, builds trust with your customers, and enhances your reputation.

- **Support local causes:** Invest in causes that are important to your community. Whether it's through charity donations, sponsoring events, or supporting local nonprofits, giving back strengthens your business's ties to its community.

- **Create jobs and opportunities:** One of the most impactful ways to give back is by creating jobs and providing opportunities for others. By offering internships, mentorships, or scholarships, you empower individuals to build successful careers of their own.

- **Sustainable business practices:** Adopting eco-friendly practices, reducing waste, or supporting sustainability initiatives can help you become a socially responsible business. Customers today value businesses that make a positive impact on the environment and society.

3. Build a Legacy

Sustaining success isn't only about financial growth; it's about leaving a lasting impact that goes beyond the business itself. A legacy-driven approach ensures your efforts continue to benefit others, long after you've moved on from the company.

- **Focus on values:** Ensure your company's values align with a greater purpose. If you prioritize social responsibility, sustainability, and community development, your business will leave a positive legacy that transcends profits.

- **Mentorship and succession planning:** As the leader of your company, one of the most powerful ways to leave a legacy is by mentoring the next generation of leaders. Plan for succession so that the business continues to thrive, even without your direct involvement.

Practical Actions to Sustain Long-Term Success

Sustaining long-term success isn't easy, but it is possible if you remain focused, committed, and strategic. Here are some practical actions you can take to ensure your business stays on top for years to come:

1. Commit to Continuous Improvement

- Always look for ways to improve your products, services, and internal processes. Stay proactive in making enhancements to stay ahead of the competition.

2. Keep Building Relationships

- Cultivate strong relationships with your employees, customers, and partners. These relationships are key to maintaining loyalty and support for your business over time.

3. Track Industry Trends

- Stay informed about industry trends and shifts in consumer behavior. This allows you to adapt and evolve your business in response to changes.

4. Create a Strategic Plan for the Future

- Continuously revisit your business strategy. Set new goals, assess progress, and adjust the plan as needed to ensure that you remain on track for long-term growth.

5. Stay Humble and Grateful

- Success is a journey, not a destination. Stay humble and grateful for the opportunities you have, and use your success to make a positive impact on the world.

Conclusion

Sustaining long-term success isn't just about keeping your business running—it's about continuing to innovate, grow, and make a positive impact. By reinvesting in your business, fostering a culture of innovation, and giving back to your community, you can ensure that your company remains relevant, respected, and successful for years to come.

Remember, success is a marathon, not a sprint. Keep pushing forward, stay committed to your values, and continue to create value for your customers, employees, and the world. In doing so, you will not only sustain long-term success but also build a legacy that will inspire future generations of entrepreneurs.

Conclusion

"Success isn't a destination, it's a journey—a journey full of challenges, opportunities, and growth. And you, my friend, are just getting started."

As you close this book and reflect on the lessons shared, I want to leave you with a final message: building a large business empire doesn't happen overnight. It's a journey—one that requires patience, resilience, and a mindset that embraces both the highs and the lows. The road to success is not straight; it's full of twists, turns, and unexpected detours. But if there's one thing I can assure you of, it's this: **you are capable of achieving great things.**

Starting your own business, scaling it, and ultimately creating something extraordinary requires persistence. There will be moments when you feel like giving up, when the challenges seem overwhelming, or when progress feels slow. But it's during those moments that the true entrepreneurial spirit emerges. The most successful entrepreneurs aren't the ones who never faced obstacles— they're the ones who kept going despite them. The ones who never lost sight of their vision and always found a way to adapt.

So, as you stand on the edge of your entrepreneurial journey, know this: **your dream of building a large business is within reach.** All it takes is a commitment to keep moving forward, no matter how tough things get.

Embrace Continuous Learning and Adaptability

In the world of entrepreneurship, there's no finish line. The business landscape is always changing, and to stay ahead, you must keep learning and adapting. The habits you build today will shape your future success. Successful entrepreneurs are lifelong learners. They read, attend seminars, talk to mentors, and constantly seek new knowledge. They know that the moment they stop learning is the moment they stop growing.

Here are a few ways to embrace continuous learning and adaptability on your journey:

- **Stay curious:** Always ask questions and look for ways to improve. If something's not working, find out why and be open to new methods or approaches. Remember, the most successful business leaders are those who remain open-minded and flexible.

- **Surround yourself with the right people:** Learn from others—whether it's mentors, business peers, or people who have already walked the path you're on. Surround yourself with people who push you to be better, who challenge your ideas, and who inspire you to keep moving forward.

- **Be open to change:** The world doesn't stand still, and neither should you. Embrace the changes in your industry, be ready to pivot when needed, and never be afraid to innovate. Your ability to adapt will be one of the greatest assets you have on this journey.

Get Started Now—You've Got This!

Now, more than ever, is the time to act. Don't wait for the "perfect moment" because it doesn't exist. There's no right time to start your business—there's only **now**. If you're waiting for the stars to align, you might wait forever. Take the first step today, no matter how small it may seem. Whether it's sketching out your business plan, researching your target market, or simply reaching out to a mentor, every action you take will bring you closer to your goal.

Entrepreneurship is about taking that first step with conviction, and then taking the next, and the next. It's about taking risks and learning from them. It's about creating something bigger than yourself, something that can stand the test of time.

Remember, success doesn't come from doing everything perfectly. It comes from staying committed to your vision, learning from your failures, and having the courage to keep going. If you've got the right mindset, a willingness to learn, and a solid strategy, you have everything you need to build your empire.

Building a Large Business Empire

Building a large business isn't just about making money—it's about building something meaningful. It's about creating value for your customers, innovating in ways that disrupt industries, and making an impact that extends beyond your company. When you start with the right mindset—believing that you can create something truly remarkable—you'll find that the journey to success becomes one of the most rewarding experiences of your life.

So, here's my final message to you: **don't wait for permission to start.** You have everything you need inside of you to make your dream a reality. Every challenge you face is an opportunity to learn and grow. Keep going, stay focused, and never give up on your vision.

You are capable of achieving extraordinary things. The road ahead may be long, but with the right strategy, mindset, and perseverance, you'll create an empire that will stand the test of time.

Get started today. Your journey to building a large business empire begins now.

"Success is not for the chosen few. Success is for those who choose to take action, learn along the way, and never stop striving for greatness."

You've got this.

References

Listed below are a number of references used to write this book as well as my personal experience.

1. Collins, J. (2001). *Good to great: Why some companies make the leap and others don't.* HarperBusiness.

2. Drucker, P. F. (2006). *Innovation and entrepreneurship: Practice and principles.* HarperBusiness.

3. Osterwalder, A., & Pigneur, Y. (2010). *Business model generation: A handbook for visionaries, game changers, and challengers.* Wiley.

4. Ries, E. (2011). *The lean startup: How today's entrepreneurs use continuous innovation to create radically successful businesses.* Crown Business.

About the Author

As author of *Entrepreneurial Power: Build Wealth and Live Your Best Life*, the author is a seasoned entrepreneur with years of experience in building and scaling successful businesses. With a passion for helping others achieve their dreams, he has navigated the ups and downs of entrepreneurship, understanding first-hand the challenges that come with turning an idea into a thriving empire.

Having built and grown companies from the ground up, he shares practical insights, strategies, and lessons learned throughout his own entrepreneurial journey. This book is a reflection of his commitment to empowering others to take charge of their destinies, make smart business decisions, and build lasting success.

Driven by a belief in continuous learning and innovation, he encourages you to embrace challenges as opportunities for growth. His mission is to inspire entrepreneurs to reach their full potential and create businesses that not only succeed financially but also make a positive impact on the world.

Welcome to your thriving and successful business empire. Embrace the journey – it is fulfilling and rewarding to challenge yourself and build success.

Darrin Elford - Entrepreneur and Certified Chief Executive Officer

www.ingramcontent.com/pod-product-compliance
Lightning Source LLC
Chambersburg PA
CBHW020419130626
46549CB00006B/2642